AMERICAN EDUCATION

. Its Men

Ideas

and

Institutions

Advisory Editor

Lawrence A. Cremin
Frederick A. P. Barnard Professor of Education
Teachers College, Columbia University

Letters On the
Free Schools of New England

James G. Carter

ARNO PRESS & THE NEW YORK TIMES
New York * *1969*

Reprint edition 1969 by Arno Press, Inc.

*

Library of Congress Catalog Card No. 77-89161

*

Reprinted from a copy in the
Harvard College Library

*

Manufactured in the United States of America

Editorial Note

AMERICAN EDUCATION: *Its Men, Institutions and Ideas* presents selected works of thought and scholarship that have long been out of print or otherwise unavailable. Inevitably, such works will include particular ideas and doctrines that have been outmoded or superseded by more recent research. Nevertheless, all retain their place in the literature, having influenced educational thought and practice in their own time and having provided the basis for subsequent scholarship.

Lawrence A. Cremin
Teachers College

Letters On the
Free Schools of New England

LETTERS

TO THE

HON. WILLIAM PRESCOTT, LL. D.

ON THE

FREE SCHOOLS OF NEW ENGLAND,

WITH

REMARKS UPON THE PRINCIPLES OF INSTRUCTION.

BY JAMES G. CARTER.

Would you have a man reason well, you must use him to it betimes.
LOCKE.

BOSTON :

PUBLISHED BY CUMMINGS, HILLIARD & CO.

HILLIARD AND METCALF PRINTERS.

1824.

DISTRICT OF MASSACHUSETTS, *to wit:*

District Clerk's Office.

BE IT REMEMBERED, that on the thirteenth day of August, A. D. 1824, and in the forty-ninth year of the Independence of the United States of America, Cummings, Hilliard, & Co. of the said district, have deposited in this office the title of a book, the right whereof they claim as proprietors, in the words following, *to wit:*

Letters to the Hon. William Prescott, LL. D. on the Free Schools of New England, with Remarks upon the Principles of Instruction. By James G. Carter.

Would you have a man reason well, you must use him to it betimes.

Locke.

In conformity to the act of the Congress of the United States, entitled "An act for the encouragement of learning, by securing the copies of maps, charts, and books, to the authors and proprietors of such copies, during the times therein mentioned;" and also to an act, entitled "An act supplementary to an act. entitled 'An act for the encouragement of learning, by securing the copies of maps, charts. and books, to the authors and proprietors of such copies, during the times therein mentioned;' and extending the benefits thereof to the arts of designing, engraving, and etching historical and other prints."

JOHN W. DAVIS,
Clerk of the District of Massachusetts.

HON. WILLIAM PRESCOTT, LL. D.

SIR,

THE deep interest you have ever evinced in whatever affects the political and moral condition of our country, has induced me to believe, you would not look with indifference upon any effort, however humble, to improve an institution of such vital importance to our happiness, dignity, and prosperity, as the system of free schools. The important relation you sustain to the first literary institution in our country, seems, moreover, to warrant in some degree my presumption, in inviting your attention to the consideration of a few general principles of instruction. It is upon these, that much of the success of all schools and seminaries of learning, however they may be conducted in other respects, must ultimately depend. The principles, I have endeavoured to illustrate, seem to me never to have been carried into effect in our country. Though my illustrations are all drawn from so humble a department as that of elementary instruction, the application will be easily made to the more advanced pursuits of literature and science.

Some of the leading thoughts in the following Letters were prepared for the press a few months since in the form of a Review; and it was not till within a *few weeks*, that I yielded to the ad..ce of friends, on whose judgment I am accustomed to rely, and determined to submit them to the publick in their present form. I have not assumed the *principles* hastily ; but the circumstances above named, together with my daily avocations, and the impossibility of examining the whole in a connected form, before it was sent to the press, may fairly claim some indulgence in the execution. In selecting your name as a medium, through which to make my communications to the publick, I was guided not merely by the reasons, to which I have already alluded. These, although sufficient to determine my choice, only came to corroborate a decision, which my personal feelings had already .suggested. With all their imperfections, and no doubt many will be detected, the following Letters are submitted to your perusal, and if found worthy, to your protection and encouragement. The highest ambition, I have dared to form in regard to them, will be answered, if they meet your approbation, and are the means of turning the public attention more to the important subject, to which they relate. I cannot, however, but indulge a secret hope, that they may be a remote cause of interesting minds more commensurate than my own, with the magnitude of the object.

Most respectfully, I remain,

Sir, your obliged and

Obedient servant,

J. G. CARTER.

Lancaster, 13 *August,* 1824.

LETTERS.

LETTER I.

SIR,

THE system of free schools in New England, has long been the subject of almost unqualified praise ; and those, who have had largest experience of its excellence, have felt themselves privileged to be most eloquent, in setting it forth to the world. The great degree of complacency, with which we dwell upon this favorite institution, has drawn upon us some illnatured remarks from our less fortunate brethren in other sections of our country. They would, no doubt, be glad to beg a truce from the subject, even at the expense of believing all that has been said. And if no object were proposed, but a vain ostentation of some little advantage, which we may happen to possess in this respect, I should spare myself the useless task of saying more upon the subject. No trait in the character of our legislation, deserves more admiration, than the liberal and high-minded policy adopted by the Federal and State

1

governments, in regard to provisions for early education. New England may well offer her most hearty congratulations, that the system of free schools, originating with her, has been introduced into most of the States of the Union ; and in some has been carried to a good degree of perfection. I am, certainly, not disposed to detract any thing from so good an establishment. It is, indeed, the richest inheritance, we enjoy from our ancestors ; and the value, we attach to it, is enhanced no small degree, by a knowledge of the sacrifices, it cost its pious founders. The first and imperious wants of a people in a " strange land," were but indifferently supplied, when provision was made by authority, for the *universal* instruction of the young. We must not analyze, too closely, *all* the motives, which induced such provision. We might, perhaps, find, that a zeal for the faith, which they believed to have been once delivered to the saints, made no small share ; for it must be confessed, that little was taught in the schools of the puritans, but catechisms containing their faith. At least, this was the grand object, and every thing else was subsidiary. The youth, who had been taught subjection to his superiors, by arguments summarily addressed to his back, and was well versed in the creed of the *then* orthodox church, was sent into the world, with perfect confidence in his competency to surmount all difficulties, which might occur in the various relations of life. But this was not long the state of things. The religious zeal of the puritans, which, to say the least, *approached* to bigotry and intolerance, was much qualified in its influence upon the early institutions of the country, by their love of civil liberty. Their political creed was hardly less heretical than their religious; and they were as impatient of control in the capacity of a body politick, as their consciences were wayward and obstinate in matters of religion. Their attachment to free institutions was devoted and enthusiastick; and they had the wisdom to discover, that "knowledge is essential to freedom." These two causes, zeal for their faith, and love of free institutions, conspiring, led to the adoption of a policy for the general diffusion of knowledge, which showed practically and efficiently, how much they loved their institutions, and how well they understood, what constitutes the basis of free governments.

New England was first granted by letters patent from King James, in 1621, to "diverse of his loving subjects," to wit; the Council established at Plymouth, and embraced that moderate portion of the American continent, "lying and being in breadth from Fourty degrees of Northerly Latitude from the Equinoctiall line, to Fourty eight Degrees of the said Northerly Latitude, and in Length by all the Breadth aforesaid, throughout the main Land from sea to sea."* One would think, by the liberality of this grant, that his Majesty did not very well understand

* Haz. Hist. Coll. vol. i. p. 105.

the geography of this continent, or that he did not set a very high value on his extensive acquisitions here. The Council of Plymouth, soon after, made large grants of territory to different companies for the purpose of settlement in New England. To Sir Henry Roswell and others, they gave the part called Massachusetts Bay ;* and this grant was confirmed in 1628, by the Colony charter from King Charles. The Colonies of Plymouth,† Connecticut,‡

* The original grant of Massachusetts Bay embraced, " all that Parte of Newe England in America, which lyes and extends betweene a greate River there, commonlie called Monomack, alias Merriemack, and a certain other River there, called Charles River, being in the bottome of a certayne Bay there commonlie called Massachusetts, alias Mattachusetts, alias Massatusetts Bay, and also all and singular those Lands and Hereditaments whatsoever, lying within the space of three English myles on the South parte of the said Charles River, or of any or everie Parte thereof; and also, all and singular the Landes and Hereditaments whatsoever lying and being within the space of three English myles to the southwarde of the southermost Parte of the said Bay, called Massachusetts, alias Mattachusetts, alias Massatusetts Bay ; and also all those Landes and Hereditaments whatsoever, which lye, and be within the space of three English myles to the Northwarde of the said River called Monomack, alias Merriemack, or to the Northwarde of any and every Parte thereof, and all Landes and Hereditaments whatsoever, lying within the lymitts aforesaide, North and South in Latitude and breadth, and in Length and Longitude, of and within all the Breadth aforesaide throughout the Mayne Landes there, from the Atlantick and Western Sea and Ocean on the Easte Parte, to the South Sea on the West Parte," &c.—[Haz. Hist. Coll. vol. i. p. 241.]

† 1629.　　‡ 1631.

and New Haven were likewise organized by char-
ters, and these four, for some time, constituted the
New England confederation. Under the Colony
charter of Massachusetts Bay, among the first legislative acts, are recorded the following characteristic
preamble and law :

" For as much as the good education of children
is of singular behoof and benefit to any commonwealth, and whereas many parents and masters are
too indulgent and negligent in that kind ;

" It is ordered, that the selectmen of every town
in the several precincts and quarters where they
dwell, shall have a vigilant eye over their brethren
and neighbours, to see ;

" First, that none of them shall suffer so much
barbarism in any of their families, as not to endeavour to teach, by themselves or others, their children
and apprentices, so much learning, as may enable
them perfectly to read the English tongue, and
knowledge of the capital laws :

" Also, that all masters of families do once a
week (at the least) *catechise* their children and ser-
vants in the grounds of religion ; and if any be unable to do so much, that then, at the least, they pro-
cure such children and apprentices to learn some
short orthodox catechism without book, that they
may be able to answer unto the questions, that shall
be propounded to them out of such catechism, by
their parents or masters, or any of the selectmen,

when they shall call them to a trial of what they have learned in that kind."*

Although laws like these would not, in themselves, lead us to form any very sanguine expectations of great progress in literature, or very astonishing discoveries in science ; yet, from the deep solicitude they manifest upon the subject, we are led to anticipate something better, as soon as the resources of the Colony are adequate to a more liberal provision. This anticipation is realized by the foundation of Harvard College in 1636. After the confederation of the Colonies, Massachusetts Bay, Plymouth, Connecticut, and New Haven, in 1643, this " school of the prophets," as it was *then* called, became an object of deep interest, and received their united and undiverted patronage.

How general was the interest taken in this institution, and how great exertions they were willing to make, for its encouragement, will appear from the following petition of the " President and Fellows," and the reply they received from the Commissioners.

" Seeing from the first evil contrivall of the collidge building, there now ensues yearely decayes of the rooff, walls, and foundations, which the study rents will not carry forth to repaire ; therefore, we present to your wisdome to propounde some way to carry an end to this worke." A reply was returned; " The Commissioners will propounde to, and improve their several interests in the Collonies, that by *pecks, half bushells*, and *bushells* of wheat, accord-

* Colony Laws, Chap. 22, Sec. 1.

ing as men are free and able, the Collidge may have some considerable yearly healp towards their occasions, and herein, if the Massachusetts please to give a leading example, the rest may probably the more reddyly follow."*

Notwithstanding the solicitude of the puritans, that the rising generation should be educated sound in the faith, as well as correct in practice, it seems, the perversity of human nature did sometimes, even in those good days, prevail; and it was difficult to find *proper* objects of the publick favour. The government of the College ask direction of the general Court, as to the distribution of their bounty in the following words.

" Whither we shall have respect, in the disposall of the said contributions, to all the schollars in generall, (as by maintenance of common officers and the like,) or especially, to such as are poore, pious, and learned ; the three *usual* qualifications looked at in such cases."† The Court reply ; " The supplies granted by the severall Collonies were first intended for the support and encouragement of poore, pious, and learned youthes, and it is desired these ends may cheefly be attended in the disposall thereof ; onely if *no such youthes* be present, it may be imployed for the common advantage of the Collidge."‡

These evidences of early attention to Harvard College are cited, not because it is that, in which I am

---

* Haz. Hist. Coll. vol. ii. p. 107.
† Hist. Coll. vol. ii. p. 85.
‡ Hist. Coll. vol. ii. pp. 86, 87.

now chiefly interested, but to show the interest, our ancestors felt on the subject of education, and the sacrifices they were willing to make for the general diffusion of knowledge. Although the College was a favorite object of patronage, the puritans did not forget the "*primary schools.*"* They bestowed upon them an attention, which evinced how well they judged, that it is *in them*, the character of the mass of the people is formed. So far as education is concerned, the highest seminaries may furnish the ornament, but the primary schools must afford the strength and stability of republican institutions. As early as 1647, less than twenty years from the date of their first charter, the colony of Massachusetts Bay made provision by law, for the support of schools at the public expense, for instruction in reading and writing, in every town containing fifty families ; and for the support of a grammar school, the instructer of which should be competent to prepare young men for the University, in every town containing one hundred families. For this exertion, which, considering the state of the Colonies at this period of their history, must have been no inconsiderable one, they assign the following truly catholick and pious reason :

" It being one chief project of Satan to keep men from the knowledge of the scripture, as in former times keeping them in unknown tongues, so in these

---

* This phrase is used to denote the elementary or lowest class of schools, which are supported by the districts of each town.

latter times, by persuading from the use of tongues, that so at least the true sense and meaning of the original might be clouded and corrupted with false glosses of deceivers ; to the end that learning may not be buried in the graves of our forefathers in church and commonwealth, the Lord assisting our endeavours :—

" Sec. I. It is therefore ordered by this Court and the authority thereof ; that every township within this jurisdiction, after the Lord hath increased them to the number of fifty householders, shall then forthwith appoint one within their towns to teach all such children, as shall resort to him, to write and read, whose wages shall be paid, either by the parents or masters of such children, or by the inhabitants in general, by way of supply, as the major part of those, that order the prudentials of the town, shall appoint : provided that those who send their children be not oppressed by paying much more than they can have them taught for in other towns.

" Sec. II. And it is further ordered, that where any town shall increase to the number of one hundred families or householders, they shall set up a grammar school, the master thereof being able to instruct youth, so far as they may be fitted for the University ; and if any town neglect the performance hereof above one year, then every such town shall pay five pounds per annum to the next such school, till they shall perform this order."* To insure the object of the law,

* Colony Laws, Chap. 78.

2

the penalty was afterwards increased to ten, and finally, to twenty pounds. And lest the moral characters of the young should suffer, by their being educated by improper instructers, this cautious and saving admonition is subjoined ; " this court doth commend it to the serious consideration and special care of our overseers of the college, and the selectmen in the several towns, not to admit or suffer any such to be continued in the office or place of teaching, educating, or instructing youth or children in the college or schools, that have manifested themselves unsound in the faith, or scandalous in their lives, and have not given satisfaction according to the rules of Christ."

As the population increased in some towns, so as to render the former provisions inadequate to their purpose, another law provided, that " every town consisting of more than five hundred families or householders, shall set up and maintain *two* grammar schools, and *two* writing schools, the masters whereof shall be fit and able to instruct youth, as the law directs." These were the laws for the support of free schools, which obtained under the Colony Charter of Massachusetts Bay, and as they were executed, they secured to all, the means of some education.

The colony of Plymouth, though not approaching that of Massachuetts in population and resources, was hardly inferior in the enlightened views entertained upon the subject of free schools. In 1667, their legislature hold the following language ; " For as much as the maintenance of good literature doth much tend to the advancement of the weal and flourishing state of societies and republicks, this court doth therefore order, that in whatever township in this government, consisting of fifty families or upwards, any meet man shall be obtained to teach a grammar school, such township shall allow at least twelve pounds, to be raised by rate on all the inhabitants." As the colony of Connecticut was principally settled by emigration from the older colony of Massachusetts, it early adopted the spirit of its laws, upon all subjects. The causes, which influenced so strongly all the early institutions of New England, operated as powerfully in Connecticut, as in any of the colonies. They *loved free institutions*, and were impatient of control from any source foreign to themselves. And their *zeal* to propagate and perpetuate a blind and bigoted *faith* was proverbial. But they did all for conscience's sake. Whatever were the causes, which led the puritans of New England to the adoption of their liberal and enlightened policy in regard to free shools, the effects were, certainly, most happy upon the condition of the people. And with the advantages of their experience, and of living in a more enlightened age, though we might wish to change some shades in their motives, we could hardly hope, on the whole, to make more noble exertions for the promotion of the same object. Their pious care of the morals of the young ; their deep and devoted interest in the general dissemination of knowledge ; and the sacrifices they endured to afford encouragement and patronage to those nurseries of piety and knowledge, *the free schools*, are without parallel in the history of this, or any other country.

LETTER II.

THE province charter from William and Mary, in 1691, ordained, " that the territories and colonies commonly called or known by the names of the Colony of Massachusetts Bay, and the Colony of New Plymouth, the province of Main, the territory called Accada, or Nova Scotia ; and all that tract of land lying between the said territories of Nova Scotia, and the said province of Main, be erected, united, and incorporated, into one real province, by the name of our Province of Massachusetts Bay, in New England." In this charter,* all grants before made to

* " Provided, nevertheless, and we do for us, our heirs and successors, grant and ordain, that all and every such lands, tenements and hereditaments, and all other estates, which any person or persons, or bodies politick or corporate, towns, villages, *colleges,* or *schools,* do hold and enjoy, or ought to hold and enjoy, within the bounds aforesaid, by or under any grant or estate duly made or granted by any general court formerly held, or by virtue of

any town, college, or school of learning, were confirmed. The laws which had been passed, under the
colony charter of Massachusetts, for the regulation
and support of free schools, were essentially confirmed, the first year after the province charter was received, by the following act of the " governer, council,
and *representatives,* convened in general court or
assembly."

" And be it further enacted by the authority aforesaid, that every town within this province, having
the number of fifty householders or upwards, shall be
constantly provided of a schoolmaster to teach children and youth to read and write ; and where any
town or towns have the number of one hundred families or householders, there shall also be a grammar
school set up in every such town, and some discreet
person of good conversation, well instructed in the
tongues, procured to keep such school, every such
schoolmaster to be suitably encouraged and paid by
the inhabitants. And the selectmen and inhabitants
of such towns respectively, shall take effectual care
and make due provision for the settlement and maintenance of such schoolmaster and masters."*

the letters patent herein before recited, or by any other lawful
right or title whatsoever, shall be by such person and persons,
bodies politick and corporate, towns, villages, colleges, or schools,
their respective heirs, successors, and assigns forever, hereafter
held and enjoyed, according to the purport and intent of such
respective grant, under and subject nevertheless, to the rents and
services thereby reserved or made payable, any matter or thing
whatsoever to the contrary notwithstanding." [Province Charter.]

* Prov. Laws, Chap. 13, sec. 4.

These, together with the subsequent provisions, that grammar schoolmasters should be approved by the selectmen of the town, and the minister of the same, or of a neighbouring town, constituted all the legislative interference, which was deemed necessary to carry into effect the whole system. Indeed, laws were hardly necessary for such a purpose, in a community so deeply impressed with the importance of the subject. The colonies of Connecticut and New Haven, zealously emulated the older colonies of Massachusetts and Plymouth, in their liberal policy for the encouragement of schools of learning and good morals. In Connecticut, every town was obliged by law to support a school for instruction in reading and writing, if the number of families amounted to fifty ; and in every county town, a grammar school was instituted. " Large tracts of land were given and appropriated, by the legislature, to afford them a permanent support."*

While the resources of these colonies did not allow them to establish a college among themselves, they contributed liberally to the support of the college at Cambridge. Frequent contributions were made for that institution, and money was paid from their publick treasury. The inhabitants, for a series of years, educated their sons at that university.† But the evil of sending their sons so far for an education, and a desire of multiplying the means of disseminating

* Trumbull's Hist. Connecticut, Vol. i. p. 303.

† Trumbull, Vol. i. p. 304.

knowledge, induced them as early as 1654, to attempt the foundation of a college in New Haven. Though much interest was excited, and some liberal donations made, yet the patronage of the colonies was too inefficient for the magnitude of the object, and all their exertions ended in the establishment of a grammar school. Connecticut and New Haven, after a series of difficulties with each other, were, at length, united in one colony. In 1700, their united exertions established Yale College at New Haven. This institution originated with the clergy, and its management was, for some time, confined exclusively to them. It early received an efficient patronage, both from private and publick munificence. The sale of one hundred and seven thousand seven hundred and ninety-three acres of publick land, granted to Connecticut by Massachusetts, at the close of a long and obstinate controversy, afforded the colony an opportunity to add six hundred and eighty-three pounds to the funds of the college.

The efforts of New Hampshire for the support of free schools, were more feeble, and suffered more interruptions, than those of Massachusetts and Connecticut. Dartmouth College,* at Hanover, had its origin from an Indian charity school in Lebanon, Connecticut. In 1770, it was removed to Hanover, and incorporated with the privileges of a college. Its

* For a more full account of the origin and early history of this institution, see Adams' History of New England, p. 508 ; and Belknap's Hist. New Hampshire, Vol. ii, pp. 349—355.

funds consist principally in lands, a great part of which are not yet productive. A college was founded in the colony of Rhode Island and Providence Plantations, at nearly the same time the college was established in New Hampshire. These institutions, together with the primary and grammar schools, which have been before described, constitute all the publick provisions for education in New England, while it remained under colonial government. There is no period in the history of our country more interesting than that, while the colonies were struggling with the difficulties incident to a new settlement, and constantly manifesting their impatience of colonial dependence. There is no trait in their policy more important in its results upon the country, than their steady and efficient encouragement of the free schools. Though liable to frequent jealousies among themselves, and involved in constant and harassing wars with the natives, and the French colonies on their northern boundary, they still carried forward with few interruptions, the great work of making a moral and enlightened people. Though each of the colonies conducted its system of schools in a manner somewhat peculiar to itself ; yet all proceeded upon the same general principle, which was to afford the means of learning to read and write, together with some knowledge of arithmetick, to every individual. With such a system, and so executed, few could be found so unfortunate as not to have learned the rudiments of reading, spelling, writing, and arithmetick.

The standard of common education, at the period of our history before the revolution, was probably not very high. But it was much, to give to *all* such opportunities, as enabled them to acquire knowledge sufficient to transact business in the common concerns of life. It was by these means, limited as they were, that a whole community were prepared to know their rights, and to appreciate the free enjoyment of them. The free schools, and the laws for their support, probably acted and reacted upon each other. The laws originating in those enlightened minds, which could foresee and estimate their effects, raised the character of the people, by the dissemination of knowledge, to such a degree as enabled them to trace their happy condition to its true source. And the intelligence and improved condition of the country, were the surest pledges, that a liberal construction would be put upon the laws for the schools. During the strong excitement, which prevailed, when the causes of the revolution were hastening on the crisis, the attention, which had been paid to the subject of education, was, probably, for a time somewhat diverted. All attention and interest were absorbed by the momentous questions in agitation, upon the result of which depended the existence of a nation. But when the independence of the country was achieved, and the Federal and State constitutions adopted, the publick attention was again turned to the system of free schools. The zeal with which they were now patronized, and the liberality with which higher semina-

3

ries were founded and· endowed, evinced that a grateful posterity were not unmindful of the treasure, which had been committed to their keeping. Since the adoption of the Federal constitution, the means of education have been vastly increased in every part of the United States. In most of the states, which have been incorporated since the revolution, reservations of land to a large amount are made for the encouragement of schools and colleges. As the settlement of the new states goes on, and population increases, these lands will be improved, and become productive. So the younger sisters of the family of the United States have resources for the dissemination of knowledge, which will increase, precisely as the population increases, and the wants of the people become more urgent. What the original states of the Union, by whose exertions and sacrifices this territory was achieved, have received as an equivalent for such copious concessions in favour of the new states, I am not able to say. Nor am I sure they have received any equivalent. But this is a question, with which I am, at present, not much interested. Whether the appropriations for education in the western states have been made by mutual and equal concessions from all the states, or whether they are made by the old states in favour of the new, the effect will be the same on the condition of those, who are to enjoy the advantages resulting from them. As the first object in the formation of every government is, to provide for its own preservation ; and as the general diffusion of knowledge and virtue is the most effectual, if not the only means of insuring stability to republican institutions, the policy of the liberal appropriations made by Congress for education, in every new state they incorporate, is undoubtedly an enlightened policy, and worthy of an enlightened and free government. In some of the states, which, since the revolution, were inhabited only by savages and brutes, schools and higher seminaries of learning are now in successful operation, affording opportunities and advantages for education adequate to prepare young men for all the professions. The means of education are not yet to be compared with those of New England ; but the time is not far distant, when in the progress of events, we may expect rivals to our free school system, in the West.

The means of education in New England have been much extended in all departments, from the primary schools up to the Colleges and University. But whether the means have been increased in as rapid a ratio as the resources and demands of the country, admits of a doubt ; or rather, it is certain they have not. Though schools, academies, and colleges, have been founded, and encouraged in all the New England States to a good degree, none have afforded so steady and efficient a patronage to them, as Connecticut and Massachusetts. Connecticut, by publick and private munificence, has built up Yale College to be the second in the Union, in the means it affords of acquiring a thorough and complete education. They have, moreover, several academies of most respectable standing, both in regard to funds, and the ability of their instructers. These afford the means of learning the languages, mathematicks, and other branches of education required for admission to the College. But the most remarkable appropriation for extending the means of a common education to all ranks and classes of people, is what is denominated the "Connecticut School Fund." This State have enjoyed several rare opportunities of providing for their schools and College. Or rather they have improved the opportunities, which every state may make for itself, if so disposed. Some appropriations for the support of common schools were made very early, but what constitutes the principal part of the "Connecticut School Fund," was obtained in 1795, by the sale of lands in New Connecticut, or what was called the Western Reserve. These lands lie in the northeastern part of the present State of Ohio. They were sold for $1,200,000. This sum by the able management of Mr. Hillhouse, the Commissioner of the school fund, amounted, according to his report, in May, 1822, to $1,700,000, in available funds.* The proceeds of this sum, amounting to somewhat more than sixty thousand dollars a year, are expended for the support of common schools. The whole State is divided into small districts, and the money has been apportioned among them, according to the

* See N. A. Review, April 1823.

amount of taxable property ; but a later law provides, that it shall be apportioned according to the number of scholars in each district.*

* By the law of the State, the several towns in it are divided into districts, for the schooling of the children and youth. Committees are appointed to examine the masters and mistresses of the schools, and take care that they are duly qualified for instructers. The State is divided, acccording to the best collection ſ have been able to obtain, into about 1580 district schools, consisting of different numbers. In some of them, there are an hundred scholars or more ; in others there are not more than twenty. On an average they will amount to fifty-five, or fifty-six. Between one third and one half of the whole population are schooled the greater part of the year—in the winter and part of the fall and spring, by masters, and in the warmer and more busy season, by mistresses. For the support of these schools, the legislature have appropriated very ample funds :—one arising from new lands, sold by the then colony, many years since— the other from the sale of the land in New Connecticut. These lands, called the Western Reserve, sold for 1,200,000 dollars. In October 1815, the value of the fund, as reported by the committee of said fund, was $1,501,914.89, secured by mortgages on lands. Since October 1815, there has been funded and added to the principal, 106,759 dollars, making the present amount of the school fund, $1,608,673 89. The dividends on the school funds, paid to the different school societies in the State for the year ending March 1st, 1818, on the list of 1816, is as follows ;

October dividend, 1817	$19,761 87
March dividend, 1818	39,643 11
Allowance of two dollars on the 1000 on the list of 1816, payable out of the treasury on the old fund,	13,174 68
	62,579 66*

* Append. Trumbull's Hist. Conn. Vol. ii. p. 547.

The effect of this fund upon the state of the schools, has not been such as might have been anticipated. Notwithstanding such ample means are afforded, exclusively for the benefit of the common or primary schools, it is questionable whether they are in any better, if in so good a state, as the same class of schools in Massachusetts. The vigilance of the people in appropriating their school money is not quickened, by laying their purses under immediate contribution; and means brought to their door, without any exertion on their part, are suffered to pass but half improved. Among other perversions of "the fund," ignorant and indifferent *instructers* are allowed to absorb a portion of it, which, under better management, could not fail of a great and a happy effect. But when the only object of this large appropriation shall be kept more steadily in view, and when the same attention and ability shall be paid to the judicious expenditure of the money, which has been paid to the accumulation of it, this State will possess advantages for educating, to a certain degree, the whole mass of the people, beyond those of any other State in the Union.

LETTER III.*

THE constitution of Massachusetts, adopted in 1780, recognises the importance of education in the following words :

" Wisdom and knowledge, as well as virtue, diffused generally among the body of the people, being necessary for the preservation of their rights and liberties ; and as these depend on spreading the opportunities and advantages of education in the various parts of the country, and among the different orders of the people, it shall be the duty of Legislatures and Magistrates, in all future periods of this Commonwealth, to cherish the interests of literature and the sciences, and all seminaries of them ; especially the University at Cambridge, public schools, and *grammar schools* in the towns."

With such a clause in the constitution, we should have anticipated some legislative provisions for education, sooner than at the end of nine years. But the institutions and system of schools, which had obtained under the Province charter, together with the exertions of individuals, were all the means en-

---

* The remarks in the succeeding letters are made with more particular reference to the schools of Massachusetts, though it is presumed, that with little variation they would be equally applicable to the schools of any of the New England States.

joyed for the diffusion of knowledge before the year 1789. In this year the legislature passed the following " act to provide for the instruction of youth, and for the promotion of good education."

" Whereas the Constitution of the Commonwealth hath declared it to be the duty of the General Court to provide for the education of youth ; and whereas a general dissemination of knowledge and virtue is necessary to the prosperity of every State, and the very existence of a Commonwealth :

" Sect. 1. Be it enacted by the Senate and House of Representatives, in General Court assembled, and by the authority of the same, That every town or district within this Commonwealth, containing fifty families, or householders, shall be provided with a school master or school masters, of good morals, to teach children to read and write, and to instruct them in the English language, as well as in arithmetick, orthography, and decent behaviour, for such term of time as shall be equivalent to six months for one school in each year. And every town or district containing one hundred families, or householders, shall be provided with such school master or school masters, for such term of time as shall be equivalent to twelve months for one school in each year. And every town or district containing one hundred and fifty families, or householders, shall be provided with such school master, or school masters, for such term of time as shall be equivalent to six months in each year ; and shall, in addition thereto, be provided with a schoolmaster, or schoolmasters, as above described, to instruct children in the English language, for such term of time as shall be equivalent to twelve months for one school in each year. And every town or district containing two hundred families, or householders, shall be provided with a grammar schoolmaster, of good morals, well instructed in the Latin, Greek and English languages; and shall, in addition thereto, be provided with a schoolmaster or schoolmasters, as above described, to instruct children in the English language, for such term of time as shall be equivalent to twelve months for each of said schools in each year."

Sect. 4. "Be it further enacted by the authority aforesaid, That it shall be and it is hereby made the duty of the president, professor and tutors of the University of Cambridge, preceptors and teachers of academies, and all other instructors of youth, to take diligent care, and to exert their best endeavours to impress on the minds of children and youth committed to their care and instruction, the principles of piety, justice, and a sacred regard to truth, love to their country, humanity, and universal benevolence sobriety, industry and frugality, chastity, moderation and temperance, and those other virtues which are the ornament of human society, and the basis upon which the republican constitution is structured. And it shall be the duty of such instructors to endeavour to lead those under their care (as their ages and capacities will admit) into a particular under-

4

standing of the tendency of the beforementioned virtues, to preserve and perfect a republican constitution, and to secure the blessings of liberty, as well as to promote their future happiness ; and the tendency of the opposite vices to slavery and ruin.

And to the end that improper persons may not be employed in the important offices before mentioned :

Sect. 5. Be it further enacted by the authority aforesaid, That no person shall be employed as a school master aforesaid, unless he shall have received an education at some College or University, and before entering on the said business, shall produce satisfactory evidence thereof, or unless the person to be employed as aforesaid shall produce a certificate from a learned minister, well skilled in the Greek and Latin languages, settled in the town or place where the school is proposed to be kept, or two other such ministers in the vicinity thereof, that they have reason to believe that he is well qualified to discharge the duties devolved upon such school master by this Act ; and, in addition thereto, if for a grammar school, " that he is of competent skill in the Greek and Latin languages, for the said purpose." And the candidate of either of the descriptions aforesaid shall moreover produce a certificate from a settled minister of the town, district, parish or place, to which such candidate belongs, or from the selectmen of such town or district, or committee of such parish or place, " That to the best of his or their knowledge, he sustains a good moral character."

Provided nevertheless, This last certificate respecting morals, shall not be deemed necessary where the candidate for such school belongs to the place where the same is proposed to be actually kept ; it shall however be the duty of such selectmen or committee who may be authorized to hire such school master, specially to attend to his morals.

Sect, 7. —————————. And it shall be the duty of the minister or ministers of the Gospel and the selectmen (or such other persons as shall be specially chosen by each town or district for that purpose) of the several towns or districts, to use their influence, and best endeavours, that the youth of their respective towns and districts do regularly attend the schools appointed and supported as aforesaid, for their instruction ; and once in every six months at least, and as much oftener as they shall determine it necessary, to visit and inspect the several schools in their respective towns or districts, and shall inquire into the regulation and discipline thereof, and the proficiency of the scholars therein, giving reasonable notice of the time of their visitation."*

This law, you will perceive, is a most alarming relaxation of the laws under the Province Charter. The provision under the coloy charter, that towns of more than five hundred families should support *two* grammar schools, and *two* writing schools, had been sunk under the Province Charter. By the statute of the " Commonwealth," towns of fifty

* Laws Mass. 1789. Chap. 19.

families are obliged to support a school for reading, writing, &c. only *six months* of the year, instead of *constantly*, as before ; and towns of *two hundred* families are obliged to be provided with a grammar school-master, instead of towns of only *one hundred* families, as under the Province law. The State was under some temporary embarrassments, soon after the close of the revolution, which is the only reason that occurs for such a departure from the policy, which had been pursued in regard to schools, from the earliest settlement of the country. The resources of the people were certainly much more adequate to the support of schools, after the establishment of a government among themselves, than while they were kept in duress by colonial dependance ; or while they were sacrificing every thing to achieve their independance. But the effect of a law, so comprehensive in the detail as the school law of 1789, cannot be estimated with great precision, without taking into account the character of the people for whom it is intended. If the law is intended to force a reluctant people to exertions *much* beyond their inclination and ability, it will probably be explained away and evaded, till it is reduced, in some good degree, to their wishes. But on the other hand, if the law indulges a relaxation from exertions, which the people have been accustomed to make, and which they have made cheerfully, realizing a full equivalent in their own condition, they will execute the law upon a construction even beyond its intention. This was the fact in the case of the school law. What the law neglected to provide for, was supplied in some degree by the exertions of individuals. The laws for the support of the *primary* free schools have never been executed upon a niggardly and parsimonious construction. The public mind upon this subject has gone much before the laws. They have followed at a large distance, rather than stimulated and controlled any interest. The towns have, in many instances made appropriations for the primary schools, of twice the sums of money necessary to answer the letter of the law. The schools provided for in the above law, are open to children of all classes, and the expense is paid by a tax on the people. Each town is made responsible for the execution of the laws within its jurisdiction. And, to give interest and efficacy to the system, it is made the duty of the minister and selectmen, or a committee appointed for the purpose, to overlook the schools,—to visit them, at least, once in six months,—to employ and approve the instructers,—and direct in the selection of school books. Although there are some instances of negligence and indifference, this duty is generally performed with cheerfulness and fidelity.

New England possesses some peculiar advantages for carrying into effect its system of education. It is divided into small townships or separate corporations of from five to seven miles square. The responsibility of these small corporations is more likely to ensure a more vigilant discharge of their duty, than if they were larger, and the subject of their responsibility less immediately under their inspection. As the population is scattered over almost the whole territory, and the children are often young, who attend the primary schools, it has been found convenient to divide each town into smaller districts for this object. Thus a school is carried to the door, or at least into the neighbourhood of every family. Each township constitutes from four to twelve districts ; and none are so far removed from all schools, that an attendance on some of them is not easy. The appropriations for schooling in each town, are adequate to support a school in each district, from three to six months in the year, and often longer. The money is raised by a tax on the *property* of the town, principally, a very small proportion arising from the *polls*. It is distributed among the districts, sometimes, in proportion to what each pays of the tax ; but oftener, a more republican principle prevails, and it is divided according to the number of scholars. There is one other principle of distribution, which is sometimes adopted, in those towns not satisfied with either of the above methods. That is, they divide the money raised as above among the districts, in the compound ratio of the number of scholars and the tax paid in such district. But this requires so much mathematicks, that even those, who acknowledge the justness of the principle, commonly content themselves to do less justice, and spare their heads the trouble of calculation.

These appropriations are expended, a part in the summer months for the advantage of the younger children, and a part in the winter months for the accommodation of those, who are more advanced in age, and whose labour cannot be spared by their poor and industrious parents. The summer schools are taught by females ; and children of both sexes, of from four to ten years attend, females often much older. In these schools from twenty to forty, and sometimes twice that number of children, are taught reading, spelling, and English grammar, by a single instructress. In the more improved of this class of schools, writing, arithmetic, and geography are added to their usual studies. In the leisure time between lessons the female part of the school, are devoted to the various branches of needlework. These primary schools, however humble the branches taught, and young the children, to whom they are taught, have a strong influence in forming the characters of the young. Although the progress in studies may be inconsiderable, yet they are important for the notions of order, decency, and good manners, which they inculcate ; and for the habits of attention and industry, which are there formed. The whole expence of a school of this kind, taught by a female, exclusive of the house, wnich in the country, costs but a trifle, does not exceed from two to three dollars per week. For this very inconsiderable sum, thirty, forty, or fifty children, are not only kept from idleness and consequent depravity, but are taught much, which will be useful to them in life. In the winter months an instructor is employed, and arithmetic, geography, and history, are added to the studies of the summer schools. These schools bring together for instruction those children and youth, whose labour is too valuable to be dispensed with, in the season which gives the agriculturist most employment. The total expense of a school of this kind amounts to from six to ten dollars per week ; and it contains from thirty to eighty, or a hundred scholars.

Such are the schools where the mass of the people must begin, and now, *end* their education. The next in order from the primary schools *were* the *grammar schools*, properly so called. These were established by the law of 1789, in all towns containing two hundred families. The object and the tendency of these higher schools were, to raise the standard of instruction, and elicit talents and genius wherever they might be found. Many through the medium of these schools have found their way to the University, and become distinguished in society, who might otherwise never have known their own powers, or thought it possible to aspire to the advantages of a public education. But this part of the system has never received that attention, which its importance demands. It has always been viewed with prejudice, and been thought to be an institution for the accommodation of a few, at the expense of the many. In many places, for want of a thor-

ough knowledge of the subject,.those for whose particular advantage the grammar schools were intended, have been most opposed to their support. The
law, therefore, has been borne with impatience,—
has been explained away and evaded,—till at length,
the prejudice has been sent into the legislature, and
the whole provision is struck out of the statute book.
At least, the remnant which remains can be of no
possible use for the encouragement of the schools.
All towns in the Commonwealth are now excused
from supporting grammar schools, except five or six
of the most populous. And these are precisely the
towns, which least need legislative interference. A
law of the legislature to oblige Boston, for example,
to make appropriations for schools, is preposterous,
when that city already expends upon the education
of its children and youth, nearly as much as the
whole remaining state. But during the series of
years, while the grammar schools have been neglected, the friends of the free schools have had an appeal to those liberal and enlightened minds, which
could better foresee the happy effects of a different
policy. And this appeal has never been made in
vain. Whenever the public interest in schools has
declined or been diverted, by the various necessities,
which press upon a people, in a comparatively new
country, it has soon been roused again, and stimulated in the proper direction. If appropriations have
not been so liberal as might be wished, those have
always been found, who would encourage the cause

by endowments for schools of a higher order. These schools or academies, as they are more frequently called, have been generally founded by individuals, and afterwards made corporations with grants of land or money from the State authorities. They have now become very numerous throughout New England. In Massachusetts, they are found in every county, and oftentimes within ten or fifteen miles of each other. They have generally been made a class above the *grammar schools*. Here, young men are prepared for teachers in the primary schools,—for mercantile life,—or for the University. This class of schools is not entirely free. The instructer is supported in part by the proceeds of funds, which have arisen from private or public munificence ; and in part, by a tax on each scholar. For the rich and those in easy circumstances, these schools answer the same, and probably a better purpose, than the grammar schools, contemplated by the late law ; but they are out of the reach of the poor. Many a poor and industrious man would spare the labour of his son, and give him an opportunity to learn, perhaps to fit for college, while the means were in his own town, who could but ill afford a considerable tax for tuition, and the price of board in a neighbouring town. This will be the effect of the repeal of the school law. The rich, at a little more expense to be sure, but that is of no consequence with them, will patronize and improve the condition of the academies for their own accommodation ; while

the poor will be left with no advantages above the
primary schools. One avenue, and that a broad and
easy one for the progress of genius in humble life,
is now shut on a large proportion of the community ;
and talents,

"Th' applause of listening senates to command,"

are doomed to a virtual death by the operation of
this measure. Its effects are the more to be dread-
ed, because they will follow their cause slowly, and
be felt most at some distant period, when it will be
most difficult to trace the evil to its source. The
means of education, though the most powerful instrument, by which a government may effect the
character of the people, are not an instrument, by
which they can produce an immediate result. As
the good to be expected from liberal appropriations,
though sure to follow, is realized to the country, only at a distance from the outfit ; so the evils of
withholding encouragement, though as sure to follow, are still at a distance. But happy experience
ought to have taught *this community*, how to estimate the magnitude of the good and evil of the different policies, even though they are at a distance.
We are now in the possession and enjoyment of
those advantages for education, purchased by the
sacrifices of our ancestors. And the question in regard to appropriations at the present day, is, whether
we shall transmit those advantages unimpaired to
posterity ; or whether we shall shut our eyes on the
future, and suffer the animating and vivifying princi-

ple of our free government to be extinguished by neglect, or perverted by a heedless and inefficient encouragement. We all profess the deepest veneration for the character of the pilgrims, and those characters, who laid the foundation of our free government ; and can we consistently depart from those traits in their policy, which have made them venerable, and our government free ? To praise the institutions and happy state of our country, and to congratulate ourselves on the free enjoyment of them, is not so much to praise ourselves, as it is to praise the liberal and enlightened policy of those, by whose wisdom and foresight we have inherited such privileges and happiness. Posterity will judge of our policy, at some future period, by its effects on *their* condition, as we now judge of the policy of our ancestors, by its effects on *our* condition. If we compare the encouragement afforded to schools and seminaries of learning, by the pilgrims of Plymouth and New England, with their resources ; and then in connexion, compare the encouragement afforded them at the present day, with our resources ; we shall be astonished and disgusted with our niggardly and parsimonious policy. We seem to rely entirely upon the liberality and munificence of individuals to redeem our degeneracy in this respect. What would our ancestors have thought of their posterity, those ancestors, who nearly two hundred years since, amidst all the embarrassments of a new settlement, provided by law for the support of *grammar schools in all towns of one hundred families,* " *the master thereof being able to instruct youth so far as they may be fitted for the University ?*" or what would our fathers have thought of their children, those fathers who, in 1780, enjoined it in their *constitution,* upon " *the Legislatures and Magistrates, in all future periods of this Commonwealth, to cherish the interests of literature and the sciences, and all seminaries of them ; especialty the University at Cambridge, public schools, and* GRAMMAR SCHOOLS *in the towns ;*" if they could have foreseen, that after one relaxation and another, in forty years, those children would so far forget their duty to " cherish the GRAMMAR SCHOOLS," as to strike them out of existence ? What the peculiar condition of the people of this State is, which renders the support of this class of schools unnecessary, impolitick, or unjust, I have never been able to understand. And, although I have been at some pains on the subject, I have never yet learned, what the arguments were, which carried the repeal of the law through the last General Court. Arguments there must have been, and strong ones, or such an alarming innovation would never have been suffered, upon an institution, to which the people, till quite lately, have always expressed the strongest attachment. Was that class of schools considered unnecessary ? If so, what has made them unnecessary ? Either the people have no longer need to receive the kind of instruction, those schools were intended to afford ; or they must receive the same instruction in some other way. The policy, and in our government, the necessity of eliciting the talents of the country, by every possible means, will be demonstrated, when we consider how many of our most distinguished Jurists, Statesmen, and Divines, have received their early instruction in the primary and grammar schools of some obscure country village. None, I believe, can be found, who will say, the people have no longer *need* of such facilities, for bringing forward to notice the promising talents of their children, and of giving to our country some of its greatest benefactors. Then by abolishing the grammar schools, it is expected the people will receive the same instruction in some other way. But two possible sources occur, which promise in any degree to supply the chasm in the system. The primary schools on the one hand,—and the academies on the other. Neither of these sources will answer the expectation, or be adequate to the purpose. The primary schools will not come up to the necessary standard, either as they are contemplated by the law, or as they are, and promise to be, supported by the people. And the academies are out of the reach of precisely that class of people, who most need the encouragement offered by the late grammar schools. The effect of the repeal of the law upon the primary schools, is as yet, but matter of conjecture. It is probably expected by some, and it is certainly to be hoped by all, that striking from the system the class of schools immediately above them, they will be improved so as in some degree to supply the place of the higher schools. If this expectation had any foundation, or if there were any probability, it would be realized in some good degree, it would not be so much a matter of regret, that the late measure was adopted. But several reasons induce me to believe, that the expectation is altogether visionary ; and that the measure will have a tendency to sink, rather than improve the condition of the primary schools. Although the late law has not been executed for some years upon a very liberal construction, yet the knowledge, that it existed, had some effect, to raise the character of instructers in the lower schools. To benefit the schools, all possible motives should be offered to raise the qualifications of the teachers. The repeal of the law has removed the strongest barrier to prevent the obtrusions of ignorance. Experience has long since proved, that the approbation of the selectmen as to the character, and of the minister as to the literary qualifications, is no sufficient check, upon the pretensions of incompetent instructers. Those, who aspire to the place of teachers in the primary schools, are very frequently found in the families of the very men, whose approbation is required. And however vigilant and candid they may intend to be, in the discharge of their duty in this respect, paternal affection is a most deceitful medium, through which a father looks upon the merits of his son. And the condition of the clergy, in the country, particularly .

at the present day, is not such as would allow us to expect from them, a very positive and decided veto in such matters, upon the pleasure of the principal inhabitants of their towns. We have now no checks, but the very inefficient one above described, to prevent the employment of incompetent instructers. And since the interest and influence of the candidate for such employment, as well as the interest and influence of his friends, will always be upon the wrong side ; it is much to be feared, that the mass of instructers, in the primary schools, will receive no other opportunities for improvement, than are afforded in the very schools, where they commence teaching. If this view of the subject is correct, the strong tendency of the present arrangement must be, to sink the condition of the primary schools. And the only, or at least, the greatest counteracting influence, which has existed heretofore, is removed, by abolishing the late grammar schools. Few towns have supported a grammar school the whole continued year, at one place. They have employed several instructers, *qualified as the law directed*, and by opening several schools of this kind at the same time, have made up the amount of a year, all perhaps, during the winter months. This evasion, which was a very general one in those towns, which took the trouble to evade at all, you will perceive, was virtually putting the grammar schoolmasters into the primary schools. The consequence has been what we should expect. Although the grammar

schools have in many places disappeared in form
and name, yet the people have a tolerable equivalent,
in the vastly improved condition of the primary
schools. Even those, who have commenced teachers from some of these schools, have possessed all
the advantage of the grammar schools, intended by
the law. The existence of the law, therefore, even
with so very inefficient an execution of it, has had
the direct tendency to improve the condition of those
schools, in which grammar masters have been employed; and an indirect influence on the other
schools, by better qualifying those who have and will
commence teachers, with no advantages above those
afforded in the common schools.

The repeal of the law obviates the necessity of
the evasion, which I have described as operating so
favourably upon the primary schools. And as the
qualifications of the instructers are diminished, the
character of the schools must decline. To this, probably, all will readily assent. But it may, perhaps, be
said, the qualifications of the instructers are as high,
for all practical and useful purposes, as they were
under the former law, as it was executed. In the
first place, it is not fair or just to reason from the
law as it *was executed*, rather than as it *should have
been* executed. In the next place, allowing ourselves so to reason, we shall not, I believe, arrive at
the same result. The qualifications of the grammar
schoolmasters, were, that they should be " of good
morals, well instructed in the *Latin, Greek*, and

English languages." This class of schools is now abolished, and " *Geography*" is added to the former qualifications of the teachers of primary schools. Allowing the two classes of schools to have been perfectly amalgamated, which is a great concession in point of fact, as well as acknowledging a great perversion of the law ; we have dispensed with Latin and Greek, and require Geography in their stead. I have no desire to lessen the estimation, in which geography is held as a study peculiarly adapted to our primary schools. And I am ready to concede, that probably ten will wish to study geography, where one would wish to study Latin and Greek. Now, if an instructer, who is qualified to teach Latin and Greek, could not by any possibility be qualified, at the same time, to teach Geography, and all the minor studies of our schools, I should consider myself as having conceded the whole argument. But this is not the fact. These qualifications are so far from being incompatible, that they *generally* exist in a superior degree in connexion with each other. The connexion, to be sure, is not so essential, that a man may not be a very good teacher of Latin and Greek, and still know very little of any thing else. Still as the studies are arranged in all our schools, academies, and colleges, where young men are prepared for teachers, all the elementary studies, including geography, are generally taught before the languages. So that by adding them to the qualifications, even if it were *never* required of the instructers to teach them, we ensure more mature and accomplished scholars in those branches, which are more frequently and generally taught. I would not be understood to discuss, much less to approve this arrangement of studies, for those destined to be scholars by profession. Such arrangement exists, and I avail myself of the fact for my present purpose. But besides ensuring better teachers for the common branches, there are always some, who would attend to the languages, as preparatory to a publick education, if they had opportunity. And if affording the opportunity to all of every town, should be the means of drawing out but few of superiour talents, even those few are worthy of the highest consideration and regard from the publick, who possess them. These and similar considerations, which I cannot here state, have convinced me, I know not whether they will convince any one else, that the repeal of the grammar school law, even if we could never hope it would be executed upon a more liberal construction, than it has been for the last ten years, will have a direct tendency to sink the condition and prospects of the primary schools.

There is one other point of view, in which the effect of the measure will be equally pernicious and equally certain. I mean its effect upon the *manners* of the scholars. This was a consideration deemed so important as to be provided for in the law of 1789. In proportion as the qualifications of instructers are lessened, it becomes easy for those to commence teachers, who have had no advantages above the primary schools. And although good manners, or " decent behaviour" have no *essential* connexion with the other accomplishments, or Latin and Greek in particular, yet they are by no means incompatible. And those, who have had the advantages of the higher schools, academies, or colleges, will be more likely to have acquired some refinement of manners, than those, who begin to teach without any preparation, except in the very place, where they have themselves been taught.

In publick and large seminaries of learning, which bring together young men from different towns, states, and sections of the country, the change in habits, manners, and feelings towards each other, is astonishingly rapid. They come together with feelings and prejudices, and oftentimes with a dialect peculiar to the different places, from which they come, and each staring and wondering at the excessive *strangeness* of the other. But a very short time loosens their local prejudices, and teaches them, that all excellence is not peculiar to any one place. The whole exterior and deportment of the young man is often almost entirely transformed, in the short space of a few weeks. The change and improvement in this respect are more rapid at first, and quite as important and valuable to him, as his acquisitions in knowledge. What has a more direct tendency to improve " the manners" and deportment of the children, who attend our schools, than to observe some refinement in their instructer ? Such is the personal influence of an instructer in a common school, that whether he is refined or vulgar, or whether he attends to the manners of his pupils or not, his manners will infallibly be imitated and copied by all, for the time, as a model of perfection. The different sections of our country are more free from dialects of the same language than any other in the world. What has produced this uniformity of language, so desirable on every consideration, but our public and common seminaries of learning,—the frequent and intimate commercial and literary intercourse between different parts of the country,—and the numerous points of contact between the educated and uneducated parts of the community ? For the interest and happiness of the whole, and especially, the lower and uneducated classes of the community, it is certainly desirable these points of contact and intercourse should be multiplied, rather than diminished. For these reasons, the employment of instructers in our schools, who have had the advantages of some publick school or college, is an object of great consideration. Besides being the most direct and effectual means, of inculcating " decent behaviour,"—of reconciling the prejudices of different parts of the country, and different classes of the community; there is still another point of view, in which the measure is not less important. It tends more than any thing else, to lessen the distance and weaken the jealousies, which very generally subsist between the educated and uneducated. The talents and acquirements of a young man of publick education are often lost to the unlettered community for some years, while they have a delicious season of mutually hating and despising each other. These evils are in some degree obviated, when, by the kind of intercourse usually subsisting between a *publick* instructer and the *publick*, they are taught by experience their mutual worth and dependence as members of the same body politick.

As the Academies are not entirely free schools, we cannot calculate upon *them* to supply instruction to the mass of the people. These are most respectable establishments, and some of them are hardly inferior in the advantages, they afford for acquiring a thorough education, to some institutions, which are dignified with the name of colleges. It is not desirable, that their condition should be impaired. Nor need any fears be entertained, that their condition will be impaired. There are enough in the community, who duly estimate the advantages of a good education, and who are able to sustain the expense of these schools, to ensure their permanent support. And as the other classes of schools, which are free, are annihilated or decline in their character and condition, the academies will be encouraged by those, who can better appreciate the advantages of good schools, and better afford the necessary expense. So far as it regards the accommodation and pecuniary interest of the rich, and those of moderate property, it is matter of indifference, whether the legislature or publick make any appropriations or provisions for schools or not. They can and will take care for themselves. These are not the classes of the community to suffer, when government withhold encouragement from the schools. It is the poor, who are to suffer. They must educate their children in *free* schools, and in their own neighborhood, or not educate them at all. The expense of tuition, of books, and of board at the academies are so appalling, as to put the advantages of those schools quite beyond the power of a vast proportion of the community. In the towns where academies happen to be fixed, the poor will of course derive some increased advantages ; but these towns are so few compared with the whole, and the incident expenses for books and tuition are so considerable, that for all purposes of directly and efficiently educating the whole mass of the people, the academies may be left out of calculation. For not one in twenty, if one in fifty, throughout the State, will ever find their way to any of them.

LETTER IV.

IF there is any one cause which has contributed more than others, to produce that remarkable degree of happiness and contentment, which pervade all classes of the people in New England, that cause is the successful operation of the system of Free Schools. The basis of the system is, that the property of *all* without distinction, shall be applied to the education of *all*. The principle and its operation were thus eloquently described by Mr. Webster, in the late convention for revising the constitution of Massachusetts. " For the purpose of publick instruction, we hold every man subject to taxation, in proportion to his property, and we look not to the question, whether he, himself, have, or have not, children to be benefitted by the education, for which he pays. We regard it as a wise and liberal system of police, by which property, and life, and the peace of society are secured. We seek to prevent, in some measure, the extension of the penal code, by inspiring a salutary and conservative principle of virtue and of knowledge, in an early age. We hope to excite a feeling of respectability, and a sense of character, by enlarging the capacity, and increasing the sphere of intellectual enjoyment. By general instruction, we seek, as far as possible, to purify the whole moral atmosphere; to keep good sentiments uppermost, and to turn the strong current of feeling and opinion, as well as the censures of the law, and the denunciations of religion, against immorality and crime. We hope for a security, beyond the law, and above the law, in the prevalence of enlightened and well principled moral sentiment. We hope to continue, and to prolong the time, when, in the villages and farm houses of New England, there may be undisturbed sleep, within unbarred doors. And knowing that our government rests directly on the publick will, that we may preserve it, we endeavour to give a safe and proper direction to that publick will. We do not, indeed, expect all men to be philosophers, or statesmen; but we confidently trust, and our expectation of the duration of our system of government rests on that trust, that by the diffusion of general knowledge, and good and virtuous sentiments, the political fabrick may be secure, as well against open violence and overthrow, as against the slow but sure undermining of licentiousness.

"I rejoice, that every man in this community may call all property his own, so far as he has occasion for it, to furnish for himself and his children, the blessings of religious instruction and the elements of knowledge. This celestial, and this earthly light, he is entitled to, by the fundamental laws. It is every poor man's undoubted birth-right, it is the great blessing, which this constitution has secured to him, it is his solace in life, and it may well be his consolation in death, that his country stands pledged, by the faith, which it has plighted to all its citizens, to protect his children from ignorance, barbarism, and vice."

From such sentiments as these, I believe there are none in this community, who would wish to dissent. As to the wisdom and policy of making *some* publick provision for the general education of the people, there has never been a doubt. But in regard to the *extent* of these appropriations, there now exists some diversity of opinion. And it is most deeply to be regretted, that those who are most timid and sceptical as to the great utility of such appropriations, seem to be increasing. At least we are left to infer this from the policy, which has been lately adopted, in regard to the schools and other seminaries of learning. Economy is emphatically the order of the day. This is well. Economy is a great political virtue, while it is economy. But when it degenerates into parsimony, and leads to a " pence calculating policy," it is not well. While the publick appropriations are judiciously expended, there is little danger of being liberal to a fault, in the means of diffusing knowledge. And it was most ardently to have been hoped, this was the last expenditure, where a retrechment would have been found necessary. There is certainly no expenditure, from which a government, especially a republican government, realizes so full and ample an equivalent, in the increased aggregate of happiness ; and none, by which

it so effectually provides for its own peace and stability. On some political measures, different classes
of the same community have conflicting interests to
balance and adjust; but in providing liberally for
schools as well as higher seminaries of learning, the
interest of all classes perfectly coincides. The rich,
upon whom the principal burden of all publick appropriations falls, have their equivalent in the improved condition of society, and the increased security of their property. How would the value of
property be impaired, and at. how dear a rate would
the rich man purchase, or save a few dollars, by suf-
fering an ignorant and naturally jealous populace to
grow up around him! a populace equally impatient
of the influence and authority, which property naturally confers, and rebellious against the salutary res-
traints of the laws. What would the splendour of
wealth contribute to happiness, if it only put the
lives of those surrounded by it, in jeopardy, by placing them between their treasures and the rapacity of
the hungry, the destitute, and unprincipled. It is
not from this quarter, that we either expect or find
opposition to liberal expenditures for education.

The middling and poorer classes find their equivalent, in having their families educated at a small expense
to themselves. For these classes of society to refuse
ample provisions for publick instruction, is virtually to
refuse to have their children educated at other's expense. Yet it is here, oftener than any where, we
find a backwardness and indifference upon the subject.

If we can suppose the small and country towns to have an interest, distinct from the large towns ; or if we can suppose the middling and poorer classes of any given town, to have an interest distinct from the rich of the same town ; the former in both cases stand with their back to the light, when they oppose, as such, public appropriations for education. Either they do not clearly understand their interest, or they completely reverse one of the safest principles to be assumed in all political reasoning. In the case of individuals, there may be some honourable exceptions in favour of human nature ; but with classes of men and nations, in order to foresee how they will act in a given case, we have only to learn, what their own *interest* will be. Now, in regard to any pecuniary appropriation for a publick and general use, it seems as plain as possible, that it is decidedly for the *interest* of the small towns in one case, and of the poorer people in the other, to advocate a large appropriation. Take for illustration the example of a bequest of publick money to the University, or any public seminary of learning, for educating indigent scholars. The two or three largest and most opulent towns in the Commonwealth will pay one half of the tax necessary to raise the required amount, and will probably not derive one tenth of the advantage of it. So the small and country towns by paying one half of the tax, may avail themselves of nine tenths of the advantage accruing from the whole. I do not pretend to great accuracy, but wish merely to illustrate the principle. In the appropriations for schools in the towns, that class of the inhabitants, who are to be the greatest gainers at the least expense, are often most reluctant at the expenditure. In this state we have no means of calculating precisely the advantage, in a pecuniary point of view, which the middling and poorer classes have in publick appropriations for schools ; because we have no returns of the number of scholars, who attend the common schools ; or of the number sent by the most opulent class. But the advantage is great. I have selected a few towns, which are fair examples of the equal distribution of property in the country, and inquired particularly into the operation of this principle. And I find that on an average about one sixth, or at most, one fifth of the legal voters in town affairs, embracing the richest men in the towns, will pay half the tax. And this same class of men, who, if they had advantage according to what they pay, would be entitled to send half the scholars, will not, on an average, send more than one sixth of them, and probably not so many. I cannot pledge myself for great accuracy here, but I am sufficiently accurate to illustrate the operation of the principle. Notwithstanding the burden of the schools comes principally upon the rich, they are the strongest advocate for their support. No one would wish the principle changed. " Government cannot subject the property of those, who have estates, to a burden, for a purpose more favorable to the poor, and more useful to the whole community. This is the living fountain, which supplies the ever-flowing, ever-refreshing, ever-fertilizing stream, of public instruction and general intelligence."* These are the aliments, which nourish and sustain free government. If they are withheld, the body politick is languid and disordered ; if they are withheld longer, a few convulsions may end its existence. Many an ardent and aspiring mind is touched at a vital point, when the means of education are withheld or perverted. Those in humble life are far removed from public observation. But if they could be heard, they would ask with an eloquence, which would touch the heart of the most calculating politician, that those means of instruction may not be farther removed, which they have so long enjoyed. Their prayers would make an argument, which none either could or would wish to resist.

Much, however, as all are disposed to attribute to the free schools, and zealously as some, and probably a majority of the community, would advocate a more liberal provision for them, it is very far from certain, that they produce all the good of which they are capable, even with their present means. Nay, it is certain, they do not. And it is much to be lamented, that means *comparatively* ample, and afforded by a community so deeply interested in their appropriation, should be misapplied, or fail of their hap-

* See Webster's Speech in Convention, on a Resolution for basing the Senate on population.

piest effect. The sketch thus far given, relates merely to the provisions of government, and the external organization of the system. And here, almost all notices of the subject, if it has been noticed at all, have rested. But, the internal organization, including the government and instruction, will present quite as interesting a view of the subject. A few remarks, therefore, upon the defects of the schools, and suggestions for improvement, will appropriately follow.

Two principal causes have operated from the first establishment of the free schools, to impair and pervert their influence. 1st, Incompetent instructers ; 2d, Bad school books. It is not a little surprising, that a public so deeply impressed with the importance of the system of schools, and so resolved to carry it into full operation, by liberal appropriations, should stop short of their purpose, and stop precisely at that point, where the greatest attention and vigilance were essential, to give efficacy to the whole, I do not mean that much good has not been realized ; on the contrary, as has been repeatedly remarked, the success of the free school system is just cause of congratulation ; but I mean, that their influence has not been the greatest and the best, which the *same means,* under better management, might produce.

I. The employment of incompetent and inexperienced instructers has probably arisen more from the peculiar situation of the country, than from any negligence or indifference on the subject. So many opportunities are open for industrious enterprise, that it has always been difficult to induce men to become *permanent* teachers. This evil, although a serious one, is one, which cannot at present be removed; but its bad effects may be more qualified, by raising the character and acquirements of instructers to a higher standard. The whole business of instruction, with very few exceptions, has hitherto been performed by those, who have felt little interest in the subject, beyond the immediate pecuniary compensation stipulated for their services. And even that has been too inconsiderable, to render a want of success in the employment, a subject of much regret. This remark applies to almost all instructers from the primary schools up to the higher schools; and it has no very remote bearing even upon some of the instructers in our colleges. Three classes of men have furnished the whole body of instructers. 1st. Those have undertaken to teach, who had no better reason for it, than that the employment is easier, and perhaps a little more profitable, than labour. No doubt many excellent instructers belong to this class. A college education is by no means essential to a good teacher of a primary school. But it must be confessed, that many of this class have been most lamentably deficient in those literary qualifications, which *are essential* to any instructer; and perhaps, still more deficient in their notions of decency and propriety, which never approach to refinement in manners. In the same degree, the schools may be made a most efficient instrument for improving and elevating the state of society when under the direction of men, who have themselves been properly taught, they may be the means of disseminating or perpetuating grossness in manners, and vulgarity, when under the direction of different characters.

2. A second class are those, who are acquiring, or have attained a publick education ; and who assume the business of instruction as a temporary employment, either to afford a pecuniary emolument for the relief of immediate necessities, or to give themselves time to deliberate and choose some more agreeable and profitable profession. This is, probably, the most useful class of instructers ; although their usefulness is much impaired by a want of experience and engagedness in the business. The thought that the employment is temporary, and that their ultimate success in life is not much affected by their success as teachers, cannot fail to weaken the motives to exertion, and discourage the sacrifices necessary to the successful teacher. The duties of the instructer are so arduous, under the most favourable circumstances, that he needs all the motives to perseverance, which exclusive devotion to the business, or self-interest can suggest. His prospects of happiness, and respectability in life, therefore, should be more identified with his success as a teacher.

3. The third class is composed of those, who from conscious weakness, despair of success in any

8

other profession, or who have been more thoroughly
convinced by unfortunate experiment, that they cannot attain distinction, perhaps even subsistence, by
any other means. There may no doubt be found
individuals among this class, who are respectable and
useful instructers. But as a class, they are the
most exceptionable of the three. To develope the
powers of the human mind, in the most successful manner, requires a discrimination and judgment, which, it seldom falls to the lot of men of indifferent talents, to possess. In the science of instruction, there is full scope for the best talents, and
the largest acquirements. All the elevated quali-
ties, either of mind or heart, which are necessary to
ensure success in any of the professions, are essential to the accomplished instructer. And some qual-
ities are required, which are not so important in any
other profession. How can he hope to arrange and
adapt the studies of a child, so as to call forth and
strengthen the different powers of the mind, in their
natural order, and in the most successful manner,
who is not capable of enumerating those powers ;
much less of analyzing them and understanding their
mutual relations and dependencies. Such, however,
is the present condition of our country, so numerous
are the demands for instructers in the primary and
higher schools, and so various are the *private interests*, which will be felt in the selection of them, that
it is, probably, too much to expect all to have the
discrimination necessary, in order to become accurate

and original observers of the phenomena of the youthful mind. But we have much to hope from those, who can better appreciate the importance of a correct system from instruction,—from the encouragement of individuals,—and the patronage of those large towns, which carry education to its greatest perfection. It is to these sources, we must look for the first examples in improvement.

There is no science, which is so difficult to be reduced to general principles, as that of education,—none where the faithful and patient induction of large experience, is so essential. Although there undoubtedly are some general rules, to which the inexperienced instructer may be referred for direction, yet these are much fewer than is generally imagined. Every mind, especially in its early development, presents exceptions and qualifications to almost every general rule, which can be adopted. So various and multiform are the phenomena of the youthful mind, so intimate the connexion, and so strong the mutual influence, of the powers of the mind, and the affections of the heart, and so fleeting and evanescent is the nature of the evidence, by which all these must be detected and classified, that he must be skilful, indeed, who presumes to offer any thing like a complete analysis. This is not now to be attempted. But from this view of the subject, it would seem, the skill of the instructer is evinced, much more in his ability to detect minute differences, and to call forth those tender and feeble powers, the evidence of which is so faint, as to admit a doubt of their very existence, than in his force to drive on the "system of things," which has been established for ages. It is as preposterous to reduce the infinite variety of young minds to precisely the same discipline, calculating upon the same result, as it would be, to hope to make all men look alike by law ; and it is as cruel as it would be to break their bodies, at once, to the bed of Procrustes. " It is one thing to learn, and another to teach. It is very possible to possess vast stores of knowledge, and not be able to impart them, even to the willing and anxious pupil. To fix the volatile, to stimulate the sluggish, and overcome the obstinate, demand an acquaintance with the human mind not quite innate, nor likely to be acquired without some experience."

II. The success of our schools depends as much on the principles,* by which thy are governed, and the school books, as on the personal and literary qualifications of the instructer. This is the sphere for useful exertion, and the source, to which we may look, for the greatest improvements. The succeeding remarks, however, are exclusively confined to the subject of School Books, and the general principles of communicating knowledge, or the Science of Instruction.

* The classification,—arrangement of studies,—and principles of government best adapted to the schools, and upon which so much of their success depends, form interesting and important subjects of discussion, on which I would gladly enter, but am obliged, at present, to relinquish the design.

Defects in the state of school and text books, are less likely to be felt, because we have all been instructed from them, and our minds are formed upon them, as upon certain models. Reformation is on all subjects progressive. Even reformers themselves cannot, at once, shake off the many associations, which obscure their judgment. And reformation, or rather improvements in the principles of instruction, are more slow and difficult to be made, than in those of almost any other subject. This is partly because the subject is one of intrinsick difficulty ; but more because so many prejudices are to be encountered. Our prejudices, however, on this subject are all honest, for they are wrought into our very nature, from our earliest infancy ; and they are the stronger, precisely, because all acknowledge the subject to be of the utmost importance, and take particular care, that all should be taught according to the most approved and philosophical plan ; that is, just as we ourselves have been taught. Every age and generation think, that they have just arrived at perfection. And they take care accordingly, that their children shall never relapse to the ignorance of their ancestors. This would be well, if they did not take almost as effectual care, that they should never be wiser than their fathers. But this is provided against with most pious care. The very best men of all ages, those, who can hardly find good enough to do, in this short life, to satisfy themselves, would, with very few exceptions, be heartily glad to freeze or petrify the world, in the perfect and consistent form, in which they are about to leave it, lest a rash and wicked posterity should jostle it out of shape.

As the principles of religion, and the principles of instruction are more important than others; so they are proportionably well guarded against all innovation, even if it should be an improvement. Every change, therefore, in either of these subjects, especially, when fundamental principles are called in question, must force its way against fearful odds. It must encounter all the deep and firm prejudices of early education,—all the authority and personal influence of our teachers,—and the almost overwhelming influence of the oldest institutions in the world.* Still every age does make some improvement upon the one before it. And though we may be insensible of the progressive motion, at short intervals; yet, at the end of a hundred years, we have left our land marks far behind.

But besides these general and honest prejudices, which no one believes he possesses, yet all do possess; there are others, in the particular case in hand, which are not entitled to so much respect. In the case of school books, there are prejudices of ignorance and interest to be encountered. The mass of

* The venerable English Universities, "Oxford and Cambridge, in the fine metaphor of Dugald Stuart, are immovably moored to the same station by the length of their cables, thereby enabling the historian of the human mind, to measure the rapidity of the current, by which the rest of the world are borne along." [Ingersoll's Discourse.]

Instructers in the primary schools, who have most influence in the selection of school books, had commonly much rather teach an old book, which they themselves have been taught, than be at the trouble of learning a new one. Indeed, so superficial has the education of most instructers of common schools been, that a new book is to them, a new subject. The particular form and words, in which the principles of any branch of learning have been expressed, and the principles themselves, are with them, identical; and if the words are varied, the principles are not recognised.

Could they be divested of all the prejudices, they imbibe from early education, it is believed the repugnance of the method, upon which school books are written, to the acknowledged principles and laws of the human mind, would be at once felt. Indeed, the whole range of text books for elementary instruction, is liable to the same remark. Since the inductive method of Lord Bacon, the sciences have undergone, and are still undergoing, an essential change. The object of pursuit, by the new system of logick, is more steadily kept in view, and facilities are added to the means of pursuit. Discoveries have, consequently, been made, which have quite transformed the whole circle of the sciences. The identity of some principles, which had been before considered different, has been established; and others have been separated, which had before been identical. Order has taken the place of confusion in all

the sciences. Chymistry has declared independence
of Natural Philosophy, and assumed the dignity of
a separate science. Political Economy has been
added to the sisterhood, and, like all young children,
bids fair to be the pet of the family.

Is it not astonishing, that, while all acknowledge
the importance of the new method of interpreting
nature, and adopt it in all their own pursuits, none
yet seem to feel, that the same principles are equally
applicable to communicating the sciences to others,
or the science of instruction? The grand principles
of instruction are much the same, they were before
the time of Bacon; but the philosophy of Mind as
well as Matter, have assumed another form. The
elementary principles of the human mind are the
same at six, at sixteen, and sixty. They exist in
different degrees of strength and improvement at different periods, and they change their relative weight,
as elements of a character; but no new power is
created, precisely at the time, the learner throws off
the thraldom of a system of discipline, calculated to
impede, rather than develop the mind, and pursues
truth in the most direct and natural way. Yet
this would seem to be the inference from the fact,
that a method of communicating knowledge is retained,
which is acknowledged to be different, and if examined, will be found to be repugnant, to the method,
the mind pursues, when left to make its own acquirements. All, who have attended in the least to
an analysis of their own minds, at the different

stages in the progress of their development, must be conscious of having to unlearn, if it may be so called, most of the acquirements of youth. That is, they must break up the arrangement and classification of their knowledge, which have been made upon a method repugnant to the principles of the mind ; and make a new classification upon the correct principle. This, all must do, whether they are conscious of it or not, who are destined to make much progress in knowledge. Although this is not so difficult a process, as might, at first, be imagined ; yet, the powers of the mind must be somewhat paralyzed in their development, and checked in the acquirement of knowledge, by the change of important principles, in the method of acquirement. The advantage of taking the correct and philosophical method at the earliest age, and pursuing it without interruption or change, can hardly be estimated. This is an achievement, which remains yet to be made ; and it is one, whose influence on the sciences, and the condition of mankind, cannot be distinctly foreseen.

The triumph of the inductive logick, although it is a cause, which has more changed the state of the arts and sciences, and consequently the whole face of the world, than any other, which has operated within the reach of history, is but half complete, till it is carried into the subject of education. The principles of the inductive philosophy should be as rigorously followed in education, as any other department of human knowledge. The school books, and we may add the text books of the colleges, are certainly not written upon the inductive method. And these are our instructers, or the models, on which our instructers form us. The books to be sure have been written over and over again, in order to keep pace with, and incorporate the improvements and discoveries in the different sciences, of which they treat. This is well, and as it should be. But the essential principle, on which they are written, is the same through all changes. This is wrong, and what should be corrected. Improvements in arrangement, and in the manner of expressing the principles of the sciences, have, no doubt, been frequently made. Indeed, the books have probably been carried to as great perfection, as they can be carried, without some more essential change in the principles, on which they have been written. They are very well executed, upon a very bad plan. The reason to be assigned for such slow progress in the improvements of school books, in particular, is a mistaken notion of the purpose of a school book ; and the fact, that there have seldom been brought to the task of elementary instruction, talents capable of comprehending, at once, the principles of a science, in their relation and dependance upon each other ; and still less capable of analyzing the powers of the young mind, to which the science is to be adapted. The books for elementary instruction, have been written or compiled, with a view to set forth the principles of the science, of which it treats, in a manner the most philosophical to those who make the books, but with little or no reference to the young minds, which are to encounter them. The object of the education, which can be given in the schools of this country, or even the colleges, is not so much to give knowledge, as to develop the powers of the mind, and strengthen them for the acquirement of knowledge, at some future period. Every thing, therefore, even philosophical accuracy, if it is necessary, must be sacrificed to the single object of adaptation to the mind. It is of little consequence, what the study is, which the child or youth is put upon, if it be so managed, as to bring forward *all* the powers of the mind, in their proper and natural order. And when the mind has acquired some strength by discipline, and a just balance among all its faculties, its attention may then be turned towards the acquirement of useful knowledge, with a good hope of success. But impatient parents have estimated instructers, by their ability to give a smattering of learning in some branch of knowledge, rather than their ability to watch over and detect all wrong associations; and to preserve the balance essential to a well disciplined mind, by encouraging or repressing different faculties as the particular case may require. Perfection of education consists more in the harmony and just proportion of all the powers of the mind, than in the overgrown strength of any one. When the plan of a school book, or the arrangement of studies generally, is such as to exercise but few or one power, this takes the lead. It monopolizes an undue share of energy, and becomes overgrown at the expense of some, or all of the other powers. The features of the mind become distorted, and unless the deformity is corrected by the judicious instructer, the effect will become permanent, and extend to the whole character.

LETTER V.

IF Socrates was said to have brought philosophy from heaven, Bacon may as truly be said to have infused it into men. The generations, that have lived between that prodigy of human intellect and ourselves, have acknowledged their obligations to him, and no doubt profited much by his instructions. But, it is apprehended, his philosophy is not yet brought down to our comprehension, and carried thoroughly and effectually into all our intellectual exertions. It is said, he felt that he belonged to a later age, than that, in which he lived ; and in anticipation of his increasing fame, " bequeathed his name to posterity, after some generations shall be passed."* Perhaps this generation is the intended heir ; and it is high time, they had put in their claim to enjoy the inheritance.

There are no means, by which we may derive more advantage from his philosophy, and consequently render more honour to his name, than by applying it to the subject of education, or the science of instruction. The applicability of his philosophy to this subject, has been, long since, acknowledged by high authority. . And the distance between the acknowledgment of the principle, and the application of it, has not been greater, than was to be expected ; especially, when we consider, that the application depended upon judgments warped by all the prejudices or " Idols" of the mind, formed under the reign of a different philosophy.

Mr. Stewart, sketching a system of logick, observes : " Another very important branch of a rational system of logick, ought to be, to lay down the rules of investigation, which it is proper to follow in the different sciences." And when, farther on, he tells us how to lay down such rules of investigation, he says : " Such is the incapacity of most people for abstract reasoning, that I am inclined to think, even if the rules of inquiry were delivered in a perfectly complete, and unexceptionable form, it might still be expedient *to teach them to a majority*

* Stewart's Dissertation on the History of Philosophy. Part i. p. 94.

*of students, rather by examples, than in the form of general principles.''** How far Mr. Stewart was able to overcome the ' Idols' of his own mind, and keep himself consistent with the principle above laid down, his book must decide.

There is a wide difference between the rules of inquiry, by which we are to proceed to the study of a science, and the principles of that science, after we have already begun to make acquisitions in it. But if the former should be taught *by examples*, the reasons are much stronger, why the latter should. It would be much easier to understand by a *maxim*, in what direction the science lays ; than it would be to understand by the same means, all the particulars or facts of that science, when the inquirer has arrived upon the ground. *The mind does not perceive a general truth, till it has perceived the particular truths, from which it has been derived.* If any thing more than our own experience were necessary to settle this point, passages might be selected from various authors, to add the weight of their authority. But it is not the custom to question this position ; and it is quite as little the custom to pay any attention to it. It is to this point, attention is now invited ; in the hope it may have, not only a speculative belief, but a practical influence upon our principles, and systems of instruction.

But this is dealing too much in generals ; or falling precisely into the error to be controverted. To

* Philosophy of the Human Mind. Introd. Part 2d. Sec. 2d.

be consistent, a particular example must be taken, to illustrate what is meant by inductive instruction. I must even be so consistent, as not to give a definition. For unless our experience upon the particular subject has been altogether similar, there would be great danger of being misunderstood, or not understood at all ; till an example explained the meaning, and then a definition would be unnecessary. After a few *examples* of the application of the principle, it will be easy for any one to make a correct definition for himself.

In selecting the example of languages, I shall probably meet more objections, and encounter more skepticks, than in any other example, which could be taken. But principles are always best tested by extreme cases. And there is no necessity for availing myself of the advantage of the happiest application I could select.

In our most approved schools, the method of teaching languages has been, to put into the hand of the pupil a grammar of the language to be taught ; and require him to learn, as it is improperly called, the general principles of the language. This is done commonly at the expense of from three to six or twelve months' time, and a thorough disgust to the whole subject. This disgust very naturally arises from being kept so long, on what he does not in the least understand.* At the end of this time, if the teacher

---

* To counteract in some degree, this baneful effect, artificial stimulants are applied. And these are increased to so intense a degree, as to produce a perfect phrenzy in the pupil, to *seem to*

has been inflexible in his purpose, and the pupil not unreasonably stupid, he will have committed to memory his grammar from end to end, including all rules and all exceptions; to which he probably attaches equal importance. He may have fixed perfectly in his memory, all the subtle refinements of all the philosophers, who have spent their lives in studying the principles and anomalies of the language; but he has made but a small approximation to a knowledge of it. This is studying the philosophy of the language before the pupil is acquainted with the facts of it.

This system of teaching proceeds upon the supposition, that the language was invented and formed by the rules of grammar. Nothing is more false. A grammar can never be written till a good knowledge of the language is attained; and then, contrary to what the pupil supposes, the grammar is made to suit the language. Now why invert this natural method in teaching language to young learners?

have learned all, that could be expected from him. Under the strong excitement of *hope* or *fear*, the young learner will spare no pains to accomplish his task. But it must be remembered, that under the influence of these motives, the object is only to convince the instructer the task is accomplished. And oftentimes the craftiness of the pupil will invent some more expeditious method for this purpose, than really to possess himself of the knowledge he is expected to gain. These short cuts to the approbation of the instructer, it is feared, are not always consistent with that ingenuousness, which it is so desirable to cultivate in the youthful heart.

Must not the facts be learned, before they can be classed under general principles? What are the *rules* and *principles*, which the pupil has *learned* at so dear a rate? They are no more than the verbal generalisation of *facts.* How have they themselves been formed? By the *experience* of those whose attention has been directed to the *observation* of the facts. They are abstract principles, the truth of which can neither be perceived, understood, nor believed, till some single instance, within the comprehension of the principle or rule, presents itself to the learner. And then he will perceive the fact in the particular case, long before he discovers its identity with the rule, if he is ever so fortunate as to discover it.

In learning the peculiarities of a language, which is but imperfectly known, the philosopher does not (although he might to much better advantage than a young learner) go to the grammar of that language; he selects the best authors and makes a careful analysis of their sentences; and thus discovers, what constructions are common with other languages, and what are peculiar to the one to be learned. At the *end* of his researches, he forms into general principles, the result of his experience. The rule, therefore, is obtained by a patient induction of particular instances, and is put in words, not to teach us anything, but to classify what has already been learned, and put it in a form convenient to be referred to, as occasion requires. As we assort our papers by

examination of each particular one, and put together the *letters* of correspondence, the promissory *notes*,
and the *deeds* of conveyance ; and then put on each
collection a label, with the title of the class, as a
convenience for reference only, not because that al-
ters the nature of the papers, on which it is put.

The analogy pursued illustrates my meaning farther.   He, who has committed to his memory all the
principles of a language, before he has had experience of the particular cases, from which those principles have been derived, will be no wiser in respect
to his language, than he, who should collect the labels of his papers, and take this for a knowledge of
their nature.   The abstract principles of a language
give no more adequate idea of the particulars, from
which they have been formed, than the labels give of
the nature and obligation of a *note*, or a *deed*, before
those papers have been separately and individually
examined.

The *facts* of a language must be first learned, and
they always are first learned, all the arrangements
to the contrary notwithstanding.   The rules in the
learner's memory are perfectly useless, till he has
learned the particulars or facts of the language ; because he cannot till then understand them.   And
when the pupil is learning the language by experience,
he will make rules for his own convenience, precisely
as a philosopher does ; and always make them as
general as his experience will allow.   As he makes
farther progress, and becomes acquainted with more

of the minutiæ of the language, he will extend the comprehension of his rules, till they become as general as the nature of the subject admits. Then the exceptions will be noticed and classed under the rules, to which they are exceptions.

Is not this natural and philosophical; and if so, why do we pursue a method diametrically opposite to both? What then is the business of the instructer? and must every pupil learn the language under all the disadvantages, which we should encounter in attempting to learn a dead language, without grammar or instructer? The business of the instructer is, to lay before his pupil those facts, which are easiest perceived. Such are the meaning of the words, and the construction of the simplest sentences. And as a knowledge of the words is attained, and the formation of the sentences understood, a principle of limited comprehension is established in the mind of the pupil, and sentences of more difficult construction are put in his way.

The duty of the instructer is more arduous; because he must know by observation, precisely how fast his pupil generalises, in order to arrange the difficulties he is to encounter. The duty of the learner is easier, and his success more certain; because he knows, if his instructer is not ignorant or careless, that he is competent to solve, of himself, every difficulty which occurs. Whereas when he proceeds to sentences and books at random, with grammar and dictionary in hand, he does not know, when he encounters a hard passage, whether it is capable of a satisfactory answer, or whether it is a subject of debate among commentators. This doubt discourages perseverance; whereas, by the other method, he knows he *can* succeed, and the responsibility is his own, if he fails. Greater difficulties, by far, are presented to the learner, in attempting to apply a principle so much more general, than his experience, than would occur in classifying the facts, only as fast as he learns them.

If this principle of teaching languages is understood, its application will be easy for instructers. A perfect development of the principle cannot be here given. It is merely suggested for consideration; and if it is found correct, philosophical, and consonant to the laws of mind; the detail will more properly follow. It may be remarked, however, on leaving the topick, that there are several methods of communicating the elements or obvious facts of a language, without even the sight of a grammar. That will come to aid in classifying the facts and knowledge of the language; but those facts and that knowledge must be attained, before they can be classified. The instructer may construe literally a few of the easiest passages or simplest sentences, which can be selected, and the learner be required to go over the same sentences by himself, till he has learned to construe them without assistance. Or, perhaps a better method would be to select some easy and interesting story, perfectly within the comprehension of the pupil, so that the interest of the piece may aid in the recollection of the words. When a very few short stories of this kind have been learned in this manner, the child may be put to construe similar pieces alone, to the instructer, who will serve as a dictionary for the words, which have not occurred before, or are not remembered. The interest of the piece confines the attention, and the meaning of the words is acquired with astonishing rapidity. The necessity of making sense of the story, will oblige the pupil directly to *observe*, that as different terminations, or certain particles are used, different shades of meaning are expressed. And he will form his experience in the observation of facts into rules, as fast as he has such experience.

Another method would be to put an easy book, with a perfectly literal translation, into the hand of the learner, and require him to learn a portion to recite without the translation. This gives a knowledge of the words, the first thing to be attained in the acquirement of a language. The particles, from their frequent occurrence, will be soon learned. And as they are supposed to be known to the pupil, the meaning of them may be left out of the translation. In the same manner, common words may be dropped from the translation, care being taken to always give the meaning of a new word, or a new sense of the same word, till it can be fairly supposed to be learned. In this manner the inflections will be better understood than in any other method. For the learner sees, at once, the different terminations, and the different relations of the words expressed by them.

During this stage with the pupil, the grammar and dictionary may be at hand, but they are to be consulted as a means of learning the lesson, and not to constitute the lesson itself. After an intimation from the instructer, that the grammar contains information, which may be useful ; and perhaps after a reference to it, by way of example to the pupil, let him consult it just as often as he pleases, and no oftener. If he does not find any aid from it in learning his lesson ; or feel the want of something of the kind, it will be of but little use, to drive him to it. But instead of wearing out some half dozen grammars, before he is advanced to any other book, and absolutely loathing the sight of one, it will be the very *dearest* book on the table. He will find all the inflections and rules laid down in the book so consonant with his own experience in the language, that he will be very much disposed to adopt that arrangement for the classification of his own knowledge.

I take geography as another example, to illustrate what is meant by *inductive instruction*. It is selected, not because it affords any peculiar advantage in the application of this method of communicating knowledge ; but because it offers a convenient opportunity to remark upon the leading principles, upon which books on the subject have been written ; and to acknowledge its increasing interest and importance as an elementary study. Children are very early capable of describing the places, mountains, and rivers, which pass under their inspection. And they commonly do it with an enthusiasm, which shows, how lively an interest they take in the subject, and how deep an impression the peculiarities of new places make upon them. When they have learned, by actual *perception*, a few of the features of the face of the earth ; at a period a little later, they are capable of feeling a similar interest in forming a *conception* of places, mountains, rivers, &c. from representation and description. Then commences the study of geography.

This is a branch of learning, which has been more neglected, than its importance deserves ; whether we consider the value of the knowledge obtained, or whether we consider the adaptation of the study, to the early development of the mind. As commerce and letters multiply the mutual interests, relations, and dependencies of distant places, some knowledge of those places becomes almost indispensable to all professions and classes of society. Till within a few years, there has been but little order or arrangement in the books, which could be studied as text books. Facts and descriptions were selected, with no very great care or attention to their importance, and with less if possible to their authenticity. These materials were thrown together upon some plan adopted from the caprice of the author, but with not the least reference to the learner. Consequently, the whole subject has been almost totally neglected. So much depends upon the *manner*, in which knowledge is presented to the understanding of the learner. But within these few years, improvements have been made, in the elementary books upon this subject, which have brought it into notice. It is now very generally, though I am far from believing very successfully, taught in our schools.

The manner of teaching it by question and answer, which is the manner adopted by the books most approved at present, is objectionable ; although it enables the young learner *to seem* to have acquired great knowledge of the subject. The questions direct the learner to the most important facts, no doubt, but that is of little consequence to him, so long as he is unable, or not prepared to comprehend them. He connects the question and its answer by some artificial association, and will repeat a passage, containing important information, with verbal accuracy. To the hearers, who have already acquired a knowledge of the subject, and who attach to the words, a definite and correct meaning, the child seems to possess an astonishing fund of knowledge. But it is apprehended, that many a child, who thus delights and astonishes his parents, and gains his book and instructer great renown, would make as sorry a figure on a more careful examination, as the child mentioned by Miss Hamilton. After answering to all his questions, and giving an accurate account of the statisticks of Turkey, on being asked

where Turkey was, a question not in the book, re-
plied, " *in the yard with the poults.*"

The improvements in our school books, upon this
subject, have consisted in greater attention and accuracy in the collection of authentick and important
facts, and in a more consistent arrangement of them.
But by far the most important improvement is the
introduction of maps. The principle of using maps,
deserves the most unqualified approbation. For when
the object and meaning of a map are thoroughly understood by the pupil, it aids him to confine his attention, and form a conception of the relative magnitude
of continents, mountains, and rivers, and of the relative situation of places, better than the most laboured
descriptions, without such aid. But the principle of
arrangement, upon which all the books upon this
subject have been written, I beg leave to object to
decidedly and strongly. The pupil is presented in
the onset, with a map of the whole world, reduced
to the size of a hat crown. In connexion with this,
he is directed to read a description of the largest
rivers, mountains, and seas ; and also to commit to
memory some account of the character and manners
of the principal nations. Perhaps he will now be
required to learn the amount of exports and imports
of the most commercial nations to the accuracy of a
farthing.

Some, not content with presenting the whole earth
to the first and single glance of the young learner, and,
as if determined to push the absurdity of the plan to the

utmost, have given the whole solar system to the child, for his first lesson in geography. This is called setting up landmarks, and getting a general knowledge of the subject; but so far from that, in my view, it is getting no knowledge at all. It is only a confusion of words, without any definite meaning attached to them.

The subject is begun precisely at the wrong end. If it is addressed to the understanding of the young learner, this arrangement seems to presume, that he will take a deeper interest in, and better comprehend the general features of the world, embracing its largest mountains and rivers, and the characters of nations, of whose existence he has never before heard, than of the roads, hills, and rivers of his own neighbourhood, and the boundaries of his own town, county, or state. Besides, he can get no adequate idea of the magnitude of the largest mountains and rivers in the world, except by comparing them with the mountains and rivers, which he has seen, and of which he has formed some definite idea.

In forming a conception of a distant mountain or river, which we have never seen, we proceed precisely as we do in forming a conception of any other magnitude. We fix upon something of the *same kind*, which is known, as a *unit of measure ;* and then compare and discover the relation of what is known, with what is unknown. So the child could form some idea of a mountain twice as high as the hill before his eyes ; or he could form a tolerable conception of a river, three times as long and as broad, as the brook, which runs before his father's door, or the river, he may, perhaps, have seen in a neighbouring town; but tell him, at once, the Himmaleh mountains in Asia, are 25,669 feet high ; and the river Amazon, in South America, extends 3500 miles in length, and empties into the ocean on the equator, from a mouth of 150 miles wide, and I am much mistaken, if he forms the least conception of what he is told.

The correct plan for an elementary geography, would begin nearer home, with a description, and if practicable, with a map of the town, in which the young learner lives. Or if that is too particular for general use, the instructer must supply the description ; and the map begin with his own county, or state, in which he will of course be most interested. From this he may proceed to his whole country or kingdom, and thence to more general divisions of the earth. The map will of course be reduced in its scale, and the descriptions grow less and less minute, as the places are farther removed ; or from any cause, are less interesting. If I have remarked with freedom on the state of books upon this subject, it has been without reference to persons, and with the single motive of inducing those authors, to whom we are already indebted for many improvements, to examine their plans, and see if one cannot be adopted, more consonant to the principles of the youthful mind.

LETTER VI.

It would be easy to multiply examples of the inductive method of communicating knowledge upon other subjects, but I shall confine myself to one more. Arithmetick deserves the place, both because it affords an opportunity to obviate some of the prejudices, which exist against it, as a study for young learners ; and at the same time, to examine the leading features of a system, already before the publick, and written upon the principle to be illustrated. Improvements in the method of teaching numbers have been more slowly made, than in any other branch of elementary instruction. This can hardly be accounted for, except that the subject has always been considered one of peculiar and intrinsick difficulties, which could not be encountered successfully, but by those few minds, favoured of Heaven, with a sort of mathematical inspiration.

Under such discouraging impressions, we need not be surprised, that no one has appeared to convince the publick by example, that the subject is not so intrinsically difficult, as has been imagined ; in fact, that it is completely level to any capacity, which can comprehend any subject. The consequence of the miserable state of the books, has been, that while all other branches have been gaining ground, and been better and better taught, arithmetick has lost, what other branches have gained; and instead of being best and most successfully taught, as its importance demands, it has been the worst, and most carelessly taught.

No adequate reason can be assigned for the declining interest of arithmetick in our schools, for the last twenty years, but the vast disparity in improvements in the books on this, and other subjects. Some variety exists in the great abundance of elementary arithmeticks, but the same general principle of communicating knowledge pervades them all. This principle is wrong. It is wrong, first, because it does not give the best knowledge of the subject; and it is wrong, secondly, because it does not afford the best discipline to the mind. These are the only purposes, for which an elementary book is studied; and a failure in both or either of these points, is capital, and fatal to the branch to be taught. The systems have been formed, no doubt, by good mathematicians, but the object of a school book, as has been before observed, is not to reduce the science to the fewest general principles, and state those principles, as a philosopher would arrange and state them for his own convenience. Adaptation to the mind, which is acquiring the science, must be ever kept in view, by the writer of a school book, which is destined to answer the only purposes for which it is written.

The plan of all arithmeticks, till quite lately, has

been, to state the principle or rule to be taught in the most concise manner possible, and then arrange under it, examples of its application. This is called the synthetick, in contradistinction to the analytic method, which begins with examples, and at length arrives at a rule. Now the first part of the process by synthesis, cannot be said to give the best, if it can be said to give any knowledge of the subject. For, what is a learner wiser after he has committed the general principle or rule to his memory ? And it is impossible for him to do any thing more, without presupposing in him some knowledge of the subject. This operation in itself can, certainly, give him no knowledge ; because it is an abstract principle, stated in terms, of which he has probably never heard. And if he has no ideas attached to the principal terms, of which the sentence is composed, he cannot understand the relation of the ideas, intended to be expressed in the sentence.

Should the learner, therefore, after committing a rule to his memory, be able to solve a question under it, the operation must be merely mechanical. He begins as the rule directs, and when he has read or said a sentence, he puts his finger upon the place, lest he should do the same thing again, and conforms literally with his direction. This done, he proceeds to read another sentence, and in like manner to comply with its direction, and at length out comes the answer. If any pupil is able to do better, than I have described, it is not because the rule, he has committed, has made him able. He has not been called upon, in this process, to exercise any *discrimination, judgment,* or *reasoning.* It would be difficult, in fact, to tell by what powers of the mind he has done it. So that, as a discipline to his mind, he has derived none, or very little advantage. The powers of the mind are strengthened only by exercise. He has acquired no knowledge of the subject, except perhaps, a greater facility in the mechanical operation. He applies a rule with as little knowledge of the principles of the science, as the man has, who works in a chemical laboratory by receipts. He forms a compound of certain elements, as directed by his receipt, and obtains the desired result. But no one would call him a chemist. This process does not constitute, or impart a knowledge of that science. That is gained only by a minute analysis of the parts, which are to enter into the compound, and the examination of their affinities for each other.

When the pupil has been worried through his arithmetick ; he is worried, because he cannot take pleasure in dwelling so long on what he does not in the least understand ; his mind is very little improved, for those faculties, which give the most decided character to a mind, have not been called into exercise. And he is hardly better prepared for the business of life, for he can neither remember the rule, nor the application of it. But the parent is satisfied, because the child has been through the book, and can repeat all the rules it contains ; and moreover, he can flourish in the application of any rule *to the examples, which are put under it*, and which his instructer has probably led him through again and again. The instructer is satisfied because the parent is; and the pupil is doubly satisfied, on both accounts. But before any of the knowledge, which has been thus attained, can be very safely put into practice, it must be learned again, and rules for the individual must be arrived at, in the only legitimate method, viz : by induction of particular examples. In confirmation of this, if it needs confirmation, we need only refer to men of business.

Who, that is actually engaged in mercantile life, thinks of applying the dogmatical rule, he has learned at school ? In the frequent occasions the merchant has for arithmetical calculations, he examines the particular case, and makes a rule for himself. In this respect the man of business is a much better philosopher, than the student, who must hunt up an analogous case, and produce his rule from a book. In this manner, the rules of a man of business will be made to correct his knowledge, and put it in a form convenient to be remembered, and not by any means to give the knowledge, as the usual method seems to intimate.

All the evils, which result from a disgust of the study, from conveying inadequate ideas of the subject, and from paralyzing in a degree, the opening powers of the mind, are removed, when it is presented in the natural and most philosophical manner. There is nothing in it peculiarly difficult. On the contrary, when presented in a form adapted to the capacity of the learner, it has peculiar interest with most young minds ; and is peculiarly calculated to call forth and strengthen their powers. On this point may be cited the opinions of some of the most acute observers of any age, of the phenomena of mind. "Arithmetick," says Locke, "is the easiest, and consequently the *first* sort of abstract reasoning, which the mind bears or accustoms itself to ; and is of so general use in all parts of life and business, that scarce any thing is to be done without it."* "Would you have a man reason well," says the same author, "you must use him to it betimes ; exercise his mind in observing the connexion of ideas and following them in train. Nothing does this better than mathematicks ; which, therefore, I think should be taught all those, who have time and opportunity, not so much to make them mathematicians, as to make them reasonable creatures."† "For," he says again, "the business of education in respect of knowledge, is not to perfect a learner in all, or any one of the sciences, but to give his mind that freedom, that disposition, and those habits, that may enable him to attain any part of knowledge, he shall apply himself to, or stand in need of, in the future course of his life." A word from Dr. Watts. "Converse much," says he, in his work on the improvement of the mind, "with those friends, and those books, and those parts of learning, where you meet with the

* Treatise on Education.   † Conduct of the Understanding.

greatest clearness of thought and force of reasoning.
The mathematical sciences, and particularly Arithmetick, Geometry, and Mechanicks, abound with
those advantages ; and if there were nothing valuable in them, for the uses of human life, yet the very
speculative parts of this sort of learning, are well
worth our study ; for, by perpetual *examples*, they
teach us to conceive with clearness, to connect our
ideas in a train of dependence, to reason with
strength and demonstration, and to distinguish between truth and falsehood. Something of these sciences should be studied by every man, who pretends
to learning."

When, therefore, we consider the influence of
arithmetical studies, in disciplining the mind; when
we estimate the utility of the knowledge to be
gained, in the transaction of the various business of
life ; and, especially, when we view the subject
as lying at the foundation of the whole science of
mathematicks ; or rather as the instrument, or key,
without which we cannot proceed to the higher
branches of the science, it rises to no small dignity
among elementary studies. To all, it is important,
to the man of business and the scholar, it is essential. There is little danger, therefore, of examining
too closely into the character of our books upon the
subject. And there is, perhaps, as little danger of
exposing too plainly the weakness and deformity of
the·bad, or of overestimating the value of the good.

The system of Arithmetick, to which I have before alluded, and which it is proposed to examine, as
I proceed, as a specimen of inductive instruction,
was published a year or two since, " by Warren
Colburn."* It is contained in two small volumes,
entitled " First Lessons in Arithmetick upon the plan
of Pestalozzi,"† and " Arithmetick, being a Sequel

* It gives me great pleasure thus publickly to acknowledge my
obligations to Mr. Colburn, not only for the light, he has afforded
me upon the subject of Arithmetick, but for what has been re-
flected from that subject to others, which have been before noticed.

† The "First Lessons" profess to be "upon the plan of Pestalozzi." Some account therefore, of this remarkable man, will
enable readers to judge, how far Mr. Colburn is indebted to him,
for his system of Arithmetick. Pestalozzi was born at Zurich in
1746. His parents were too obscure for him to inherit much
consequence or notice on their account. He early became interested in the subject of education, and viewing the miserable condition of the lower classes of the people in his neighbourhood,
he resolved to devote himself to elementary instruction, as the
most direct and effectual means of improving their situation and
prospects. From the time he commenced instructer, he was so
exclusively devoted to his employment, that he seemed to live
only for that object.

He made bold innovations upon the established principles of
instruction, and probably on that account, did not at first receive
such notice, as his exertions merited. But the ardour of his interest was not cooled by neglect. The aid of a few friends, who
were attracted by the reasonableness of his principles of instruction, and an inefficient patronage from the government of his
Canton, enabled him to establish a school, which gave some ce-
lebrity to his name, and at length gained the assistance of some
very warm and able friends. Pestalozzi was at length united

to First Lessons." Waving here the question of in-
dependent authorship, which Mr. Colburn might
with some propriety claim, I shall enter, at once, in-

with Mr. de Fellenberg, who from similar motives had established a school at Hoffwyl. This school has attracted considerable
notice in Europe, and has been approved, and encouraged by
some of the most distinguished men of the age.

The object of Mr. de Fellenberg was, to find a plan for the
education of the poorer classes of society, at the least expense.
Agriculture, therefore, constituted an essential part of the education. But the principles of government and instruction, adopted at his school, succeeded so well, that pupils were sent from
many of the principal families in every part of Europe. In con-
junction with, and under the patronage of Mr. de Fellenberg,
who was a gentleman of some fortune, Pestalozzi was enabled to
carry his improvements in the principles of instruction, into
more complete operation. It would be foreign to my present
purpose, however interesting the subject, to go into the detail of
that establishment. We are interested, at present, only in the
method of instruction.

It was a fundamental principle in their system, never to suffer
a pupil to pass over, what he did not thoroughly comprehend.
The course of instruction was so conducted, as to give accurate
and well defined ideas upon the subject to be taught. For this
object, the instructer gave lessons in the field ; and upon subjects, which there presented themselves. This manner excited
and kept up a lively interest in the learner, because he saw at
once the use and application of what he was learning. The instructer was thus spared the perplexing question, " cui bono ?"
which so constantly arises in the pupil's mind, and which can so
seldom be satisfactorily answered. " Questions continually occurred respecting the measures of capacity, length, weight, and
their fractional parts ; the cubic contents of a piece of timber,
or a stack of hay, the time necessary to perform any particular
task, under such or such circumstances, &c. &c." The boys en-

to an examination of the general principles of the system; it being a much more interesting question, *what* the system is, than *whose* it is. The system

deavoured to find the solution of arithmetical and mathematical problems without writing, and at the same time to proceed with the mechanical process, in which they might happen to be engaged.

This method of instruction, among improvements in other branches, gave rise to the plan of Arithmetick, invented by Pestalozzi. He began with the most simple combinations upon small numbers, and proceeded to the more difficult, as the learner acquired strength to encounter them. The language of figures, and their use in the solution of questions involving large numbers, were reserved for a later and more difficult stage in their progress. These hints constitute the principal assistance, which Mr. Colburn derived from Pestalozzi, in forming his system of Arithmetick. He has adopted the arrangement of Pestalozzi in some of the combinations, but he has rejected it in others, and developed all, by the selection and composition of examples, in which he derived no assistance from him. Pestalozzi undoubtedly discovered the applicability of the *inductive method* to communicating knowledge, whether he knew it by that name or not, and applied that method in teaching the science of numbers. Mr. Colburn, with hints from him, has applied the same method to teaching the same subject, but in a manner somewhat peculiar to himself. Both, in common with all the philosophers since Bacon, are indebted to him for telling them how to *learn*, and how to *teach*. And it would, perhaps, be better if Mr. Colburn would say at once, " Arithmetick upon the plan of Bacon," rather than adopt any name, which can only reflect, what it has received from him. The identity of the principles of this method of instruction, with the inductive method of acquiring knowledge, taught by Bacon, has never been established and inculcated by those, who have adopted the method as a basis for their books. [For a more full account of the establishment at Hoffwyl, see Ed. Rev. Oct. 1819, and Simond's Switzerland. Vol. ii. pp. 193, 194 and 330—340.]

is new, and widely different, from any thing before published in this country. These circumstances, together with the importance of the subject, and the happy illustration, it affords, of inductive instruction ; seem to require a pretty detailed account of it ; I shall confine myself, however, in my remarks, merely to general principles, except so far as detail is essential to their illustration.

The distinctive traits in the character of the system will be at once seen, by examining it under the following principal divisions—

I. It teaches all the combinations in Arithmetick, with numbers so small, that the mind of the pupil can perfectly comprehend them.

II. Every new combination is introduced by practical examples upon concrete numbers.

III. All those rules, which are merely artificial, and those formed for particular applications of the same general principle, have been discarded.

The first principle above stated gives rise to the division of the subject into the " First Lessons" and " Sequel." The solution of every arithmetical problem requires two processes ; first, to analyze the question and determine the relation of the several numbers ; and then to reason upon those numbers, in a manner peculiar to the science, till the result required is attained. These two processes must be performed in the solution of every problem ; but when the numbers are so small, as not to require the aid of a written numeration, they are both performed together. That is, the relations of the numbers are discovered, at once, as fast as in the analysis, they are compared with each other.

This division of the subject has never, to my knowledge, been made, in any system of arithmetick, published in this country. And in consequence of presenting both processes in a combined form at first, neither has been very perfectly learned; and the reasoning, which is the more imp tant, both as a part of arithmetick, and as a discipline to the mind, has been least understood. At the age arithmetick is first put into the hands of a learner, the importance of having him attain clear ideas of his subject, can hardly be estimated. If a habit is contracted at this period, of being satisfied with loose, shadowy, and ill defined ideas, it will exercise a strong and pernicious influence, through the whole course of his education ; and perhaps produce a decided cast in the character of his mind. To counteract this habit, and form the contrary one of attaining distinct ideas, and reasoning clearly upon every subject, the learner must be presented with such processes of reasoning only, as that he can perfectly comprehend every step in the process. This can be done in the science of numbers, only, by giving examples of reasoning upon small numbers, till the mind acquires sufficient strength to encounter more complicated combinations upon large numbers.

The power of attention, which is so essential to every mind, and which it is so difficult for the young mind to acquire or control, is more improved by arithmetical calculations, than by almost any discipline, which can be offered. And when it is once acquired by the study of numbers, it may be easily transferred to other studies; and thus all the sciences derive an advantage, from the increased strength of a power, which few or none have so happy a tendency to improve.

The " First Lessons" introduce and inculcate every principle in arithmetick, by a collection of examples, although not a rule is given in the book. It must not be imagined, however, that a mere collection of examples constitutes an inductive arithmetick. To a superficial observer, it would seem no very difficult matter, to bring together examples to any extent. And if this were all, that is essential to a complete and successful induction, it would, indeed, be easy, and quite within the power of any one, who has sufficient patience. But this is the least and the lowest of the efforts necessary to accomplish such a work. The mind of him, who would undertake to make a book of this kind, with any rational hope of success, must be capable to take in, at one view, the whole subject. He must resolve, without any reference to existing books, arrangements, or rules, the whole science into its first and essential principles. And be able to comprehend these, in all their relations and dependencies upon each other. For they cannot be successfully developed, except in the order or such dependence.

And when by the exercise of no common share of acuteness, these elementary and essential principles are arranged in their natural order; the mass of examples must be carefully examined and assorted, for the development of each principle, and for each combination of principles. The work is still but progressing. The examples thus assorted according to the principles involved in them, must be again examined and arranged with reference to the young mind, which is to encounter them. A neglect or failure in this point would be as fatal as in any other. From this view of the subject, it would seem no humble labour, to produce a consistent book upon such a plan. And the author may congratulate himself, and the publick may well congratulate him, if he gets through such a work, without making some, nay, many mistakes.

Upon this plan, the pupil learns the reasoning, and not the technical name for it. And, I am much mistaken, if the child or youth, who has carefully analyzed every example in this little book, (which claims to be only first lessons,) and found the answer in his own way, has not a better knowledge of fractions in all their combinations, and in fact, of every principle of arithmetick, than it would be possible for him to gain, by reading the most elaborate treatise on the synthetick plan. The little reasoner will not dare to say he has learned Addition, Subtraction, Multiplication, and Division; Interest, Single Rule of Three, and Double Rule of Three; for he has probably never heard of half these terms. But propose him a question under either of those rules, involving only numbers within his comprehension, and he will analyze the problem, and perform every operation in the solution distinctly, and give you the correct result. And if he is called to it, he will explain the *why* and *wherefore* of every step in the process.

Now, when parents leave off insisting, that their children's memories shall be burthened with a confusion of rules, which they do not in the least understand, and which it requires all the energy of the young mind to retain ; and when they become contented, that their powers of mind are developing in their natural order, and as fast as the God of nature intended they should be developed, we may expect this subject to become more interesting to young learners, and to be more scientifically and successfully taught.

After the power of attention is strengthened, and habits of discrimination and analysis are in some degree formed, by examples on small numbers ; the next thing to be learned is, a knowledge of the arbitrary signs or figures, and their use in facilitating our reasoning upon large numbers. This is taught in the " Sequel," which adds what is necessary to complete the science of arithmetick. The " Sequel" is divided into two parts. The first contains examples only ; and those arranged, as in the " First Lessons," in the order of their dependence upon each other.

And if the principles, by which the examples are to be solved, have no dependence, they are arranged in the reversed order of the difficulty a learner will be likely to encounter, in their solution. This arrangement enables the learner to bring the increased strength of his mind, at each advance, to bear upon the more difficult parts of his subject. The second part contains an analytical development of the principles, and is to be studied in connexion with the first. When the learner has performed the examples in the first part, which involve a principle, he is turned to the second part, and there sees the same principle developed in an abstract form, till at length he arrives at a *rule*, which he can now comprehend, because he has learned all the variety of particular examples, to which the rule is applicable. The rule is now, no more than a verbal generalisation of what he has already learned : and it is the last thing he arrives at in order, instead of the first, as in all other systems. The separation of the examples, and the analytical development of the principles, into two separate parts of the work, is arbitrary, and not at all essential to it, as a specimen of induction. It would be as convenient for the pupil, to arrive at his rule at the end of his examples, as to be turned to a different part of the book. Although in this form, it would be more difficult to see, at once, the outline of the subject.

The method of putting the examples before, and as a means of arriving at the rule, is undoubtedly the correct one, for all subjects, which are to be learned by induction ; but all subjects are not so to be learned. The language of arithmetick, including notation and numeration, is not a subject to be learned by experience. The signification of the digits, 1, 2, 3, &c., is arbitrary, and the laws, by which they are used in reasoning upon numbers, are arbitrary. The meaning of figures, and the laws, by which they are used, are agreed upon by arithmeticians, and he, who approaches the subject of arithmetick, must first be initiated into the meaning of the signs and symbols peculiar to the science. Mr. Colburn's system in one instance, violates this principle. It requires the learner to write in words, examples of large numbers expressed in figures, before it teaches him numeration. It would be impossible for a learner to " write in words 270,000,838,103,908," before he had been told the meaning of these signs, and the laws, by which they are made significant of different numbers, as they occupy different places.

In the corresponding article, in the second part, Mr. Colburn has given the subject a thorough investigation. And I have never seen so intelligible a treatise on numeration as is there contained in a few pages. It may be suggested to him, to make some different arrangement, in the future editions of his book, by which this departure from the plan of never presenting a difficulty, which the learner is not competent to surmount, shall be remedied.

LETTER VII.

THE second distinctive characteristick of the inductive system of arithmetick, which I proposed in
the preceding letter to examine, is this ;—*Every new
combination is introduced, by practical examples
upon concrete numbers.* This, together with the
principle of always beginning with numbers so small,
that the mind of the learner can perfectly comprehend them, constitute an essential part of what is
peculiar to the inductive system. The resonableness
of the principle above laid down, will be more appa-
rent, when I have attempted an analysis of the process
of abstraction performed in the mind of a child in its
first attempts to reason upon numbers.

Abstraction is one of the last, as well as most difficult processes, which the young mind performs. The
plan, therefore, of introducing every new combination,
by examples upon *concrete* numbers, is the dictate of
sound philosophy. It has its origin in the phenomena
of the human mind, and is consonant with their general and acknowledged laws.

Perception is a power earlier developed in the mind
of a child, than conception. It is much easier, to
attain the *perception* of an object, which is presented
to the senses, than to form a *conception* of the same

object, when it is withdrawn from their cognizance. The importance of calling out the tender powers of mind by judicious discipline, in the order nature has pointed out, has never been, and hardly can be sufficiently estimated. The science of numbers is an abstract science ; but the first ideas of number must be derived from things. And nature has made three pretty distinct steps, in the process of abstracting the numbers from the things, to which they are always at first attached. The first, when the objects are present to the senses, to which the numbers to be reasoned upon are applied. The second, when those objects are absent from the senses, and the mind must form some conception of them, as something to which to attach the numbers. The third, is what is properly called abstraction, and loosens, if it may be so called, the numbers from every object; and the mind reasons upon *them*, without reference to anything existing.

To follow the course, which nature has pointed out in the development of the mind, these steps in the process of abstraction should be kept distinct, by exercising the learner upon them in the order, in which they rise from each other. For this reason, it is important that the child, in its first essays to reason upon numbers, should always have some external objects, to which he may attach his numbers, present to the senses. This stage in the science of numbers, a science, which by one abstraction and generalisation after another ends in Algebra and the higher branches of Mathematicks, is level to the capacity of a child, almost as soon as he can speak. This approach to reasoning upon abstract numbers, although it is one of the best exercises, which can be offered to a young mind, has never been made a part of mental discipline. The fault has been, in some degree, supplied by chance and the natural propensity of the mind to proceed philosophically in its acquirements. In a more correct system of discipline for very young learners, this desideratum cannot fail to be supplied. Exercises in calculation by means of sensible objects, have a most salutary influence upon the mind of a child. They confine the attention, and quicken the perceptions, at an age when it is most difficult to select employments, which do not involve powers of the mind not yet developed.

The second stage in the process of abstraction, or forming a conception of absent objects, to which to attach numbers, and reasoning upon the numbers, in this connexion, is the one, with which this system introduces all the combinations in arithmetick; " care being taken to select such examples, as will show the combination in the most simple manner." The attention is confined during the reasoning, by attaching the numbers to a vivid conception of absent objects, and the feeble powers of the youthful mind, are thus enabled to go through a process of reasoning, which could not otherwise be endured.* The

* I do not notice the Maps, which accompany the system as taught, both by Pestalozzi and Colburn, because I think them of

application of this combination may then be put to the pupil, in some example involving large numbers, with a more rational hope,.that he will better understand, both what he wishes to do, and the means of doing it.

This principle of introducing new combinations with concrete numbers, has never before been carried into arithmetick. But an analogous principle is recognised in studying Geography by maps, and Astronomy by a globe or orrery. These helps only aid the mind, in forming a conception of the relative magnitude of rivers, mountains, and the heavenly bodies, from description. The same principle is recognised in all our attempts to make an abstruse and difficult subject, understood by others. If we wish to explain any transaction between several men; we immediately suppose *you* to be one of the characters, *him*, another, and *myself*, a third ; and thus by the aid of these sensible objects, we can explain any complicated transaction between three men.

at least doubtful utility. When the pupil has reasoned by them a time, and learned to solve questions upon them, he is required all at once *to suppose them to vanish*, and reason upon the numbers without them. But the association will have become so strong, that this abstraction will cost more trouble to the pupil, than if in his progress, he had used a variety of objects for the purpose ; thus learning by example, that the objects, by which he reasons, may be constantly changing, while the reasoning remains precisely the same. This enables him to form the abstraction with less difficulty. I have not been able to test this part of the system by experience, and therefore, pronounce upon it with more hesitation.

If a jurist, for example, wishes to explain the legal descent of property through different branches of a family, to one not familiar with the subject, he does not state the principle in an abstract form, using all the technical terms of his profession, which would be precisely analogous to the common method of teaching numbers ; but he immediately presses the whole company into his service. He supposes this man, a son ; another, a brother ; a third, a grandson, and so on, till he has represented every branch of the family by some present person ; and then in connexion with these persons, he illustrates his principle clearly, and the supposed family resume their former relations, with a perfect knowledge of the abstract principle to be communicated.

This method of communicating an abstract principle, is just as applicable to elementary arithmetick, as any other subject ; and it is even more important in this application, than any other. No processes of reasoning for children are more complicated, than those of arithmetick. There are none, where the young mind requires more helps, to enable it to pursue its course, without distraction or interruption. Is it not because this facility in communicating knowledge has not been applied to arithmetick, that that study has been pronounced intrinsically difficult, and far beyond the capacity of young learners ? And with this impression, the whole subject has been wrapt in mystery as unintelligible, as the hieroglyphicks of the Egyptian Magi.

14

This improvement will ultimately give to arithmetick its proper rank and dignity, among elementary studies. The third stage or abstraction, properly so called, loses sight altogether of any particular objects, and the mind reasons upon the numbers alone. This is where all have, heretofore, taken up the subject. And the evils of the method have been long and severely felt.

The third characteristick, which I proposed to examine, it will be recollected, is the following :

All those rules, which are merely artificial, and those formed for particular applications of the same general principle, have been discarded. Such rules make the largest, and by far the most difficult part of the common systems of arithmetick. Any arrangement, therefore, by which they disappear in form and name, will seem, to superficial observers, to change the identity of the subject. But such may be assured, that notwithstanding the great transformation in the *looks* of arithmetick, the whole subject remains.

The arrangement of the system by analysis and induction is according to *principles*, and not according to *subjects*, as in other books.*

A thorough knowledge of general principles, and the habit of analyzing, which this system is so em-

* Mr. Colburn shall state his own arrangement. " In tracing the principles, several distinctions have been made, which have ot generally been made. They are principally in division of whole numbers, and in division of whole numbers by fractions,

inently calculated to give, will better prepare the mind for the examples which occur in life, than the multiplication of complicated rules, so nearly alike, that much discrimination is required to distinguish them. The rules of Barter, Loss and Gain, Fellowship, Equation of Payments, and Alligation are not recognised by name, according to this arrangement. But the principles necessary to the solution

and fractions by fractions. There are some instances also of combinations being classed together, which others have kept separate.

" As the purpose is to give the learner a knowledge of the principles, it is necessary to have the variety of examples under each principle as great as possible. The usual method of arrangement, according to subjects, has been on this acount entirely rejected, and the arrangement has been made according to principles. Many different subjects come under the same principle; and different parts of the same subject frequently come under different principles. When the principles are well understood, very few subjects will require a particular rule, and if the pupil is properly introduced to them, he will understand them better without a rule than with one. Besides, he will be better prepared for the cases which occur in business, as he will be obliged to meet them there without a name. The different subjects, as they are generally arranged, often embarrass the learner. When he meets with a name with which he is not acquainted, and a rule attached to it, he is frequently at a loss, when if he saw the example without the name, he would not hesitate at all.

" The manner of performing examples will appear new to many, but it will be found much more agreeable to the practice of men of business, and men of science generally, than those commonly found in books. This is the method of those that understand the subject. The others were invented as a substitute for understanding." [Sequel, preface, pp. vii. and viii.]

of questions, usually put under these rules, are fully illustrated. The learner finds himself solving all such questions, with the utmost facility, in the most philosophical manner, without even knowing, that such rules exist by name. I subjoin a few examples of questions, solved by the complicated and artificial rules of the most popular books, and then add the same questions solved by analysis. Readers shall then judge, which method is most expeditious and philosophical.*

* I select examples from an " Arithmetick, by Daniel Adams, M. B." because they are fair specimens of the common method, and because this book has been more generally adopted in New-England, and more widely circulated over the whole continent, than any other. Between 1802 and 1815, " it had been through nine editions, and more than 40,000 copies of it had been circulated." At that time, it was stereotyped, and I fear my knowledge of numeration would not enable me to state the numbers, with which the publick have since been afflicted. This book owes its popularity precisely to that trait in its character, which ought, in the onset, to have condemned it to oblivion. It degrades the whole *science* of arithmetick to a mechanical *art*. As a discipline to the mind of the learner, therefore, it is useless, and worse than useless. It calls into exercise no power of the mind, but memory, and requires the practice of no virtues but *faith* and *patience* : faith to believe all that is stated, for nothing is analyzed or proved; and patience to labour so long in the dark, without ever understanding, or coming to the light. The principles of the science, the development of which constitutes the chief excellence of any system, cannot be disentangled by the learner, from the useless forms, in which they are involved. The pupil never thinks of any thing but doing his " sums," and getting through the book. It is difficult to dwell with any complacency or patience on the fact, that so many of these books

A man bought 12 cords of wood at 3 dollars per cord, and paid for it with flour at 6 dollars per barrel. How many barrels of flour did he give?

It seems necessary to beg my readers not to spoil my illustration, by solving the above problem at once, before they have been taught to do it *by rule.* In the first place, this question belongs to a rule called " Barter," and it is proper they should *commit to memory* a definition of Barter. Here it is. " *Barter is exchanging one commodity for another, and teaches merchants*" (I suppose no one else has a right to know it) " *so to proportion their quantities that neither shall sustain loss.*"

When this definition is well committed, my readers are permitted to learn *by heart,* the following

RULES.

" 1. *When the quantity of one commodity is given with its value, or the value of its integer, as also the value of the integer of some other commodity to be exchanged for it, to find the quantity of this commodity :*—Find the value of the commodity of which the quantity is given, then find how

have been so long suffered to waste and pervert the precious time of those, who have but little time, at most, to bestow upon the subject. The public are intreated to look into the claims of this book to such overwhelming patronage ; and to examine it thoroughly, both in regard to the knowledge it gives of the subject, and the discipline it affords the mind. For nothing but a misapprehension of the subject,—of the purposes of a school book,—and the principles of the human mind, will excuse the mischief, it is allowed to do the community.

much of the other commodity, at the rate proposed, may be had for that sum.

"2. *If the quantities of both commodities be given, and it should be required to find how much of some other commodity, or how much money should be given for the inequality of their values:* —Find the separate values of the two given commodities, subtract the less from the greater, and the remainder will be the balance, or value of the other commodity.

"3. *If one commodity is rated above the ready money price, to find the bartering price of the other :*—Say, as the ready money price of the one, is to the bartering price, so is that of the other to its bartering price."

Now under which of the above cases does the question come? Here I leave my readers in the midst of the difficulty ;—and without wasting time in tracing analogies, solve the question without any reference to a rule. Twelve cords of wood, at three dollars per cord, will cost thirty-six dollars, and it will take as many barrels of flour, at six dollars per barrel, as there are sixes in thirty-six. There is no great trouble in arriving at an answer.

I shall not regret obliging my readers to learn so much mathematicks, at such an expense of patience, if I convince them *by example* of the trouble of it; and may assure them at the same time, this is precisely what thousands and thousands of learners in our schools, are doing every day. An example involving small numbers, only, was selected to make the illustration more plain. The reasoning would be the same, however large the numbers. The same difficulties are experienced in numerous rules, but this single example will suffice to expose the difficulties and suggest the remedies.

Could I enter into a detailed examination of the execution of the inductive system of Mr. Colburn, much would be found, to show a profound knowledge of the subject, as well as of the powers and principles of mind, to which it is adapted. A few faults might be detected by a vigilant and scrutinizing eye. But as I am obliged, by the circumstances under which I write, to confine myself to general principles, and forbear to enlarge upon the excellencies in execution, justice requires me to abstain from the faults.

LETTER VIII.

THERE is one result from the arrangement of arithmetick by general principles, so important, that it demands particular consideration. The Rule of Three is entirely omitted. Those, who first learned arithmetick mechanically, and have never thought of it except in connexion with its forms, will start at so bold an innovation; and think of course, that a rule, which has been dignified with the name of the Golden Rule, and which takes up with all its modes, no inconsiderable portion of their books, cannot be omitted, without omitting something essential to the subject. This is not the fact. The omission is an essential improvement. But this is being positive without proof. Objections will, no doubt, be started. So far as they can be anticipated, they shall be met under the two heads of the *possibility*, and the *expediency* of the omission.

First. It will be possible to dispense with the rule, if all questions which are now solved by it, can be solved by other rules, or by general principles. This is a position pretty easily sustained. I offer four examples, which present all the variety that can occur under the Golden Rule.

The first is an example of the "Rule of Three Direct;" the second, of the "Rule of Three Inverse;" the third is an example of direct proportion in "Double Rule of Three;" ánd the fourth, of "Inverse Proportion," of the same rule.

1. If a family consume $\frac{4}{5}$ of a barrel of flour in 3 weeks, how many barrels would they consume in 15 weeks?

Analysis. If they consume $\frac{4}{5}$ of a barrel in 3 weeks, they will consume one third as much, or $\frac{4}{15}$ of a barrel, in one week; and if they consume $\frac{4}{15}$ of a barrel in one week, they will consume 15 times as much, or $\frac{60}{15}$, equal to 4 barrels, in 15 weeks.

2. If 3 men do a piece of work in 7 days, how long will it take 5 men to do the same work?

Analysis. If 3 men do the work in 7 days, it will take one man three times as long, or 21 days ; and if it take 1 man 21 days, 5 men will do the same work in $\frac{1}{5}$ of the time, or $\frac{21}{5}$ of a day, equal to $4\frac{1}{5}$ days.

3. If the interest of $50 for 2 months is $3, what will be the interest of $30 for 5 months?

Analysis. If the interest of any sum of money for 2 months, is 3 dollars, the interest of the same sum for 1 month will be $\frac{1}{2}$ as much, or $\frac{3}{2}$ of a dollar ; and if $\frac{3}{2}$ of a dollar is the interest of $50, the interest of 1 dollar will be $\frac{1}{50}$ as much, or $\frac{3}{100}$ of a dollar ; if $\frac{3}{100}$ of a dollar is the interest of 1 dollar for 1 month, the interest of $30 will be thirty times as much, or $\frac{90}{100}$ of a dollar, and for 5 months it will be 5 times as much, or $\frac{450}{100}$, equal to $4,50.

4. If 8 dollars' worth of provision serve 7 men 5 days ; how many days will 16 dollars' worth of provision last 4 men?

Analysis. If any quantity of provision will serve 7 men 5 days, it will serve one man 7 times as long, or 35 days ; if 8 dollars' worth serve one man 35 days, one dollar's worth will serve him but $\frac{1}{8}$ as long, or $\frac{35}{8}$ of a day, 16 dollars' worth will serve him 16 times as long, or $\frac{16 \times 35}{8}$, equal to 70 days ; and the same provision can serve 4 men but $\frac{1}{4}$ as long or $\frac{70}{4}$, equal to $17\frac{1}{2}$ days.

15

These examples of analysis, which are spread out to their full length, demonstrate the entire practicability of solving, upon general principles, every question, which can occur under the rule of single or compound proportion. Small numbers were selected, only, because the analyses would be better understood; the reasoning would be the same, however large the numbers.

Secondly. It will not be *expedient* to omit the form of the rule of three, unless the substitute offered is more *expeditious*, more *philosophical*, and better *adapted* to the future progress of the learner, in the higher branches of mathematicks. 1. While the numbers involved in questions of the rule of three are small, the calculation will always be carried on in the mind, without any reference to the form the rule prescribes. If the numbers are large, the question must be examined in the same manner, and when it is sufficiently understood, to know what operations are necessary to discover the relation of the numbers, the learner may as well proceed, forthwith, to the solution, as to make a parade of proportion; for every step in the solution is as essential after the statement as before. Placing the numbers in a line with a certain number of points among them, is altogether arbitrary. It would be just as well to place the numbers in the corners of the slate or paper, and then multiply the numbers in diagonal corners, and divide by the odd number, and put the quotient, or answer, in the other corner. Indeed, if the form of proportion is to be considered useful or essential, this arrangement is preferable on some accounts. It does not lead the pupil to suppose the truth or answer is elicited, somehow, slyly, by virtue of those little dots, he puts among his numbers.

2. The method of solution upon general principles, is more *philosophical;* because in the operation, the mind is intent only on discovering the relation of the numbers; whereas, in the formality of a proportion at length, the attention is divided between circumstances and forms, which are of no importance to the solution, and those principles which are essential. That method cannot be called philosophical, which fixes the attention on a *form,* and induces neglect of the only part of the process, which is important. Besides, if the form must be presented, it is made more artificial and unphilosophical, in all the popular books, than is necessary. A common method is; " State the question by making that number, which asks the question, the third term, or putting it in the third place; that which is of the same name or quality as the demand, the first term; and that which is of the same name or quality with the answer required, the second term." This rule gives explicit directions for a mechanical operation; for all the knowledge of the principles of the rule, the pupil gets by it, he might as well have learned *hocus pocus.* Take an example, and state it by the rule.

"If 9lbs. of tobacco cost 6s. what will 25lbs. cost?

OPERATION.

lbs. s.   lbs.

As 9 : 6 : : 25 to the answer.

    25

   ——

    30
    12

   ——

9)150(16s. 8d.
   9

   ——

    60
    54

   ——

    6
    12

   ——

9)72(8d.
  72

  ——

    00

Here 25lbs. is made the third term according to the rule, by being put in the third place, for no better reason than because it asks the question, (what will 25lbs. cost?); 9lbs. being of the same name is the first term; the 6s. must occupy the remaining place.

Now "multiply the second and third terms together and divide by the first." Why? My readers can probably tell; but it is very certain, that the youth, who is just entering upon the subject, can assign no better reason for it, than because the rule says so. He has no more conception of what this step, in particular, has to do with obtaining the answer, than the natives had of Columbus' means of predicting an eclipse. And he ought to be as much astonished if he gets the true answer, as they were, when the event hap-

pened according to his prediction. If this is philosophy, I do not understand what that term means. I
should call it catching the truth by legerdemain.

To assign as a reason for such statement, that the
"first term has the same ratio to the second, as the
third has to the fourth," is, if possible, more unphilosophical. It is not only ridiculous, but absurd. A
ratio, that is, any ratio, which relates to the rule of
three, is the number of times one quantity is contained in another of the same kind. It is just as absurd
to talk of the ratio of pounds weight, and shillings, as
it would be to talk of buying a week of salt, instead
of a bushel; or a yard of wine instead of a gallon.
A ratio subsists between the figures, which express
the number of units in one quantity, whatever be the
unit of measure, and the figures, which express the
number of units in another quantity, however different the unit of measure. That is to say, 5 is equal
to 5, and is half 10. No one doubts this ; but when
the numbers are made concrete, by attaching to
them particular denominations, it becomes absurd
to say, 5 pecks are equal to 5 days ; or that 5 pounds
are half of 10 yards. This absurdity, which dis-
gusts the learner, if he is sufficiently inquisitive to
ask for reasons for what he is doing, is avoided, by
a solution upon general principles.

The same question solved by analysis, would be
reasoned upon thus. If 9lbs. cost 6s., 1lb. must cost
$\frac{1}{9}$ as much, or $\frac{6}{9}$ of a shilling ; and if 1lb. cost $\frac{6}{9}$ of a
shilling, 25lbs. will cost 25 times as much, or $\frac{25 \times 6}{9}$,

equal to $\frac{15}{9}$ of a shilling. In this method, although essentially the same operations are performed upon the numbers, the pupil understands the reason of every step, and can tell, precisely, what approach he makes by it, to the true answer. Whereas, by the formality of a proportion, he does not know the object of any particular step. He only knows that by performing certain mechanical operations, he obtains an answer like the book. The proportion is a sort of crucible, into which he throws his numbers, and by a process altogether as unintelligible to him as shaking the crucible, he gets the desired result. He has no means of knowing whether the result is correct, but by comparing it with the book. But by analysis, he has intuitive knowledge at each step, and is as certain of his conclusion, as he is that two and two are four.

3. But one objection more can be anticipated to the system of arithmetick, which discards the formal rule of three. The doctrine of proportions has been considered very important, if not essential to the higher branches of mathematics. And all the books upon Geometry and Algebra, and all which treat of their application to the physical sciences, are filled with them. They are not only made the great instrument of reasoning; but they constitute of themselves, in all their modes and forms, a great part of all systems of arithmetick, geometry, and algebra. It is certain, a scholar would not be able to read the books on the higher branches of the pure and mixed

mathematics, without a knowledge of proportions, at least, sufficient to translate them into more intelligible language. But the French mathematicians, who have pursued the science more successfully than any others, for the last century, have long since pro- .nounced the *formal* proportion unnecessary. Lacroix, who *understands* the subject of mathematicks, if he does not the best method of teaching it, after stating the doctrine of proportions in all their modes and forms ; says, " This theory was invented for the pur- pose of discovering certain quantities by comparing them with others. Latin names were for a long time used to express the different changes or transforma- tions, which a proportion admits of. We are begin- ning to *relieve the memory* of the mathematical stu- dent from so *unnecessary a burden ;* and this parade of proportions might be entirely superseded by sub- stituting the corresponding equations, which would give greater uniformity to our methods, and more *precision to our ideas.*"*

Clearness and precision in our ideas are important on all subjects ; on the subject of mathematics, they are essential. On moral questions, we balance prob- abilities, and found our belief on a preponderance of evidence ; but in mathematics, we have demonstra- tion or nothing. If one step in the process of dem- onstration comes short of intuitive knowledge, the demonstration is destroyed. Here, then, a want of clearness and precision, is a want of knowledge. And

* Lacroix's Alg. Camb. Edit. p. 231.

if abolishing the parade of proportions will give *more precision*, it is certainly desirable, that they should be struck out of our books. The object is so important, and the effect so certain, that the improvement must ultimately prevail. The only reason why they have been retained so long is, that no one wishes the trouble of writing over again all the books. Proportions hold their place in the mathematical books, precisely by the same tenure, which retains radical signs as a means of expressing roots in algebra. No one, who has attended to the subject, will doubt, that fractional exponents are a much more convenient and intelligible method of expressing the same thing. Still the change in the books would be so very considerable, that no one has yet undertaken to suppress radical signs. The manner of representing the truth may be totally indifferent to adepts in the science, but to one just entering upon the subject, it is highly important. He has enough to encounter in the difficulties of the science, without being embarrassed by an unintelligible language. And when more just views are entertained of the importance of adapting the science to the capacity of the learner, there can be no doubt, that both these improvements will find their way into the mathematical books. The temporary evil of changing the mode of expression is, surely, no sufficient reason for retaining what is acknowledged an obscure and troublesome notion. And if the change is ever to be introduced, it must be begun in the very first books, which are put into the hands of children.

I am now done for the present, with the principles of instruction. If any apology is due for the length, to which the discussion has been protracted, that apology will be found in the importance of the subject. The principles, which have been stated and illustrated, have a most important bearing upon existing books and systems of education. If they are correct and philosophical, there are some great and radical defects, which are intimately interwoven with our best plans for instruction, and which call loudly for attention and reformation. Although the principles have been acknowledged by high authority ; it is not upon that, they must mainly depend. Are they consonant with the known phenomena and laws of mind ; and will they stand the test of the touchstone of experience ? If so, they are worthy to be adopted ; if not, they ought to be rejected. If we estimate authority by its antiquity,—if principles are to be received with meek submission, according as they have held a sway longer and wider over the opinions of men, the odds are fearfully against us. But this reverence for antiquity, which it is almost profanity to question or violate, although it proves a salutary check upon rash innovation, is also a troublesome barrier against wholesome improvement. How else is it, that amidst the vast improvements in all other sciences, the science of instruction remains so stationary, upon the ground it occupied, two thousand years ago. The empire of mind has been widely extended, both over itself, and over the material world. But the progress is still slow. Bacon has thrown forward an anchor, with which the world have not yet come up. And if our scholars and philosophers will consent to seize hold and pull, they will produce a much more sensible motion, than to be hoisting their sails and flourishing their pennants in a dead calm.

The science of instruction is the sphere, and our country is the place for free and unembarrassed exertion. Hope certainly gives us a bright and animating prospect in the distance. The subject of education has never excited so deep and lively an interest, in every part of our country, as at present. If this interest can be directed by the wisdom and experience of the more enlightened, it cannot fail of a great, and a happy effect. The *importance* of the subject has long since been felt; the time has come, when attention should be turned to the *nature* of it. We may then hope for those improvements, of which the subject is susceptible; and those splendid results in the state of society, which the more ardent and philanthropick anticipate. But science now sits solemn in her temple afar off. The ways of approach are dark and devious. A few votaries, only, by chance or untired perseverance gain access, till at the expense of half their lives, they are warned by experience like an inspiration from above, to become as little children, that they may enter. But when the

influence of education is more duly estimated; and
when the cultivation of the head and heart, shall be
united, and form one distinct and dignified profession,
drawing to its practice the greatest and best of men;
we may then hope a proper direction will be given
to the opening minds, and expanding hearts of the
young ; and that all the deep and permanent prepos-
sessions of childhood and youth, will be upon the
side of truth and virtue. Science, philosophy, and
religion will then be blended with their very natures,
to grow with their growth, and strengthen with their
strength. The whole earth will then constitute but
one beautiful temple, in which may dwell in peace, all
mankind ; and their lives form but one consistent
and perpetual worship.

The distance of the author from the press has prevented our submitting for his correction all the preceding letters, as they were struck off. This will account for a few errors, which might not otherwise have escaped. PUBLISHERS.